Crochet A-B-Sea

AN EXTRAORDINARY UNDERWATER ALPHABET

PONY MCTATE

TO TIGER, MY LOVE
You gave me your heart
and 60% of your wardrobe space for yarn storage.

My thanks.

First published in 2018

ISBN 978-0-473-44895-0 (softcover)

Copyright © Pony McTate // All rights reserved. Don't be a plonker: no part of this publication may be reproduced in any form or by any means, electronic or mechanical, by photocopying, recording or otherwise, without prior written permission from the author.

The author has made every effort to ensure that all the instructions in the book are accurate and safe, and therefore cannot accept liability for any resulting injury, damage or loss to persons or property, however it may arise. It is the responsibility of the reader to ensure that any items made using these patterns are safe for young children.

www.ponymctate.com

CONTENTS.

5	Introduction		35	Kelp

PRELIMINARY STUFF

- 8   Abbreviations
  Things You'll Need
  About This Pattern
  About This Book
- 9   Difficulty
  Yarn
  Measurements
  Gauge/Hook Size
- 10   What You Can Make

TECHNIQUES

- 11   Magic Loop
  Rnds: Work Neater Seams
- 12   Back Loops/Front Loops
  Fasten Off: Invisible Join
  Decreasing
  Weaving in Ends
- 13   Changing Colour
  French Knots

THE PATTERNS

- 16   Background Square
- 17   Anemone
- 18   Blobfish
- 20   Clownfish
- 22   Deep Sea Angler
- 24   Electric Eel
- 25   Flying Fish
- 27   Great White Shark
- 29   Humuhumunukunukuapua'a
- 32   Inexplicable Shrimpgoby
- 34   Jellyfish

- 35   Kelp
- 36   Loggerhead Sea Turtle
- 38   Manta Ray
- 40   Narwhal
- 42   Octopus
- 44   Porcupine Puffer
- 46   Quahog
- 47   Red Crab
- 49   Sea Slug
- 51   Tube Worms
- 53   Urchin
- 55   Vampire Squid
- 57   Walrus
- 59   Axolotl
- 61   Yellow Tang
- 63   Zooplankton

FINISHING OFF

- 68   Blocking Your Squares
  Sewing Down Creatures
- 69   Attaching Fabric Backing
- 71   Joining Your Squares
- 72   Working The Border
- 73   Using The Creatures

ADDENDUM

- 76   Colours Required
- 79   About Pony

INTRODUCTION.

It's handy being a crocheter. There's no problem it can't solve. Cold? Just whip up a scarf. Bored? Fill the void with rows of meditative stitches. Local park benches looking a bit drab? Yarnbomb your way to urban renewal. So, when a friend of mine announced she was happily pregnant, I knew what to do. Thoughtful and heartfelt, a crochet baby gift would tick all the boxes.

That was how the A-B-Sea blanket started out.

Just a simple crochet make, I thought. Something useful made of joined squares, perhaps with a nice little fish stitched on the corner.

That idea percolated away for a while until one night — ping! — I sat bolt upright in bed with the plan for an alphabetical sea creature blanket. I was so excited. It would be accurate, educational, awesome. With wiggly bits to fiddle with. I would forgo the obvious in favour of the odd. That meant goodbye dull old dolphin and hello deep sea angler. A porcupine puffer for P! And for the letter I? Maybe a... hmmm... well, I'm sure I'd work it out later. (Much, much later, as it turned out. You would not *believe* how few sea creatures start with I, let alone crochetable ones).

So I got a bit carried away. You know that magical feeling, when undiluted creative energy is singing through your veins? Oh, it was glorious. Midnight sessions with encyclopedias and strange forays into the obscure world of hardcore fish fanciers. Hours spent perfecting a pectoral fin. The project took on a life of its own in the most wonderful way. I learnt much about the mating rituals of manta rays, among other things.

When I posted pics of the blanket online, other people loved it too. Righto, I thought, I'll publish a pattern to share with you all. And here it is, in a nice big book you can rest your cup of tea on (you eReaders will have to use your imagination). What I really love about these patterns is their versatility. If you're up for a big project you can make the whole blanket. Or, less ambitiously, you can pick and choose your favourite squares to make into a cushion. Or play around with the creature motifs (they make nifty gifts). My favourite square is the Zooplankton one, though the Tube Worms — which almost broke the internet — will always have a special place in my heart. What about you? What's your favourite square?

I hope you enjoy them all.
#CrochetABSea

Before You Begin.

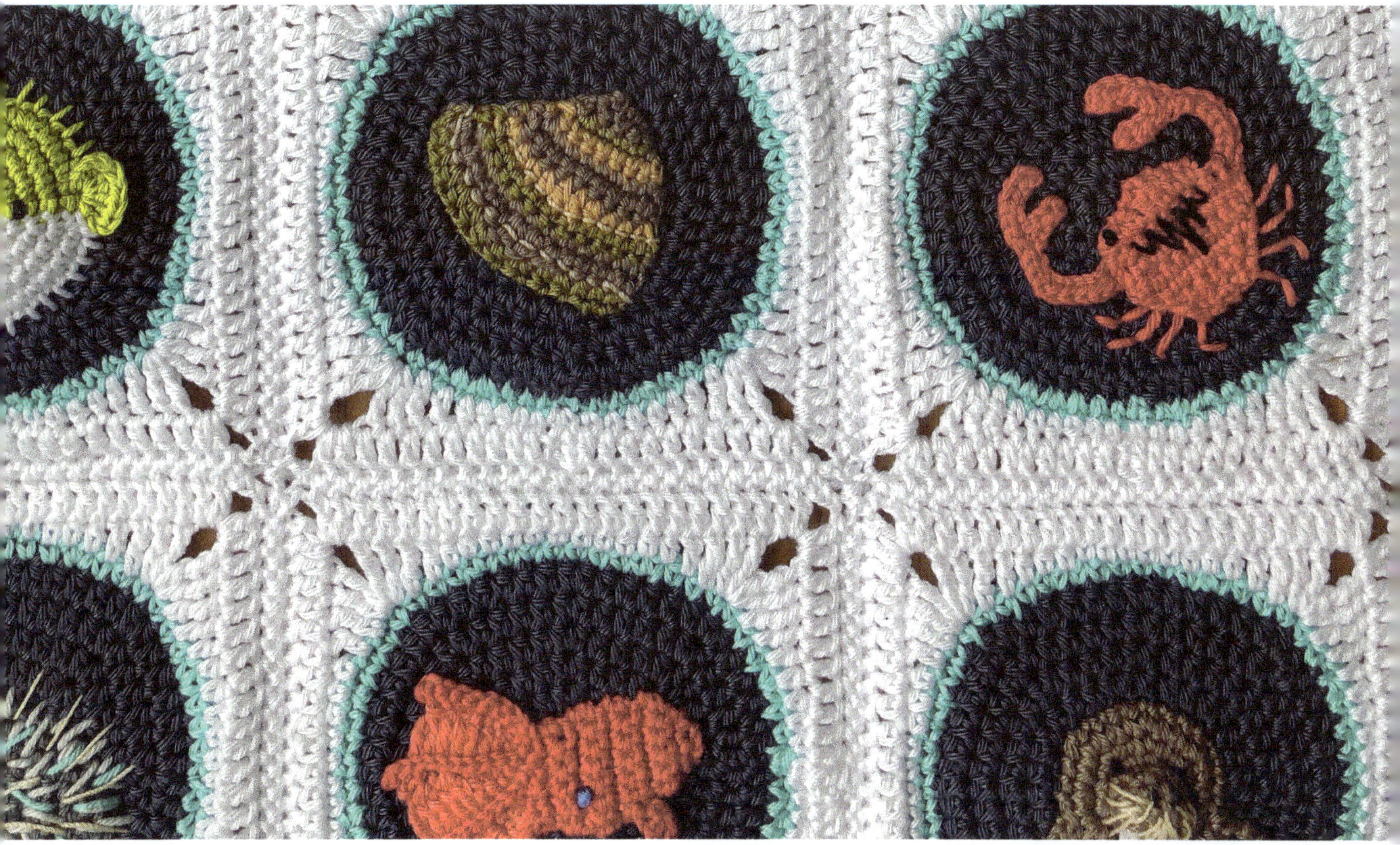

PRELIMINARY STUFF.

ABBREVIATIONS — UK TERMS.

BLO	back loops only	**rnd(s)**	round(s)
ch	chain	**RS**	right side
dc	double crochet....................US = single	**sl st**	slip stitch
dc2tog	dc 2 sts together/decrease	**st(s)**	stitch(es)
dtr	double treble........................US = treble	**tr**	treble................................US = double
FLO	front loops only	**WS**	wrong side
htr	half treble....................US = half double		

THINGS YOU'LL NEED.

- **A 3mm (C/2 or D/3) hook** for the background squares, creatures and the border.
- **A 4mm (G/6) hook** for the seams.
- **Yarn**: Scheepjes Catona and Scheepjes Maxi Sweet Treat — see *Yarn* on page 9.
- **Tapestry needle**
- **Scissors**
- **Polyester stuffing (optional)**: you can add dimension to your creatures by inserting a pinch of stuffing when you sew them onto their background squares. Or use your leftover yarn scraps.

For the fabric backing:
- **Soft fabric**: I used lightweight cotton sweatshirt material.
- **Tailor's chalk**
- **A cup or bowl** around 9.5cm (3¾in) in diameter to use as a circle guide.

ABOUT THIS PROJECT.

This book will guide you through crocheting your own A-B-Sea blanket. The blanket is made up of 30 squares and features 26 appliqué sea creature motifs — one for each letter of the alphabet. You can use the creature motifs independently to make cool embellishments as well.

The patterns are written in UK terms. Techniques are explained with photo diagrams and there is an abundance of step-by-step photos throughout.

The background squares are worked in rounds. The creatures are worked flat separately and then sewn onto the completed background squares. Finally, and to hide your stitches, a circle of fabric is blanket-stitched onto the backs of the squares. The squares are joined with double crochet seams then finished with a simple border.

ABOUT THIS BOOK.

The crochet techniques used in this book are all thoroughly explained first, with photos. You'll find the pattern for the background square comes next, then the patterns for the 26 individual creatures. At the back are the instructions you'll need for finishing your squares, such as sewing down the creatures, attaching the fabric backing and the pattern for the border.

READ THROUGH ALL THE INSTRUCTIONS BEFORE YOU BEGIN.

But you knew I was going to say that, didn't you? Honestly, it'll help.

DIFFICULTY.

The patterns in this book are written for an intermediate-level crocheter, or an adventurous beginner. It assumes you already know the basics of crochet stitches and how to read crochet patterns. But you will find lots of help throughout the book.

Some of the creatures are trickier than others. To give you can idea of what you're in for, look for the starfish in the *Notes* section of each pattern:

 EASY
Straight-forward, simple shapes.

 MODERATE
Several elements, some embroidery.

 COMPLEX (but totally do-able)
Fiddly, tricky colour changes, lots of embroidery.

YARN.

Your A-B-Sea blanket is made with **Scheepjes Catona** fingering weight cotton yarn (100% mercerised cotton, 50g/1.8oz, 125m/137yds). Some creatures also feature embroidered details using **Scheepjes Maxi Sweet Treat** laceweight cotton yarn (100% mercerised cotton yarn, 25g/0/8oz, 140m/153yds).

The list of colours you will need is a long one, but don't be put off. Catona yarn comes in smaller ball sizes (25g and 10g) as well as the usual 50g balls (and a 100g ball for the main white colour used throughout). For those colours used only occasionally throughout the blanket, a smaller ball will suffice.

Each pattern sets out the colours you need. The full list of colours and quantities you will need is set out in the *Addendum* on page 76.

As a general guide, you will need:
- Catona 50g: 11 ball
- Catona 10g: 19 balls
- Maxi Sweet Treat 25g: 4 balls

You won't use much Maxi Sweet Treat so you'll have plenty left over. You could substitute for Catona colours instead but your detailing won't be as refined.

MEASUREMENTS.

Each square measures 12cm x 12cm (4¾ in x 4¾ in). Gauge isn't critical but it will, of course, impact the final size of your blanket and how much yarn you use: see *Gauge/Hook Size* below.

The completed blanket measures 70cm x 82cm (27½in x 32¼in). This makes it roughly stroller size.

But there are loads of other ways you can use your squares and creatures too. For some inspiration, see *What You Can Make* on page 10.

GAUGE / HOOK SIZE.

The background squares, the creatures and the border are all worked with a 3mm (C/2 or D/3) hook. For the seams, jump up a hook size to a 4mm (G/6). This gives you a looser even tension and stops the seams puckering.

After Rnd 7, the centre circles of my background squares measure 8.5cm (3¼in) across.

It isn't critical to match my gauge but if you don't, it will affect the size of your finished blanket and the amount of yarn you use. Keep this in mind if your gauge is different to mine. Adjusting your hook size can help. If your circle is bigger than 8.5cm (all you Loosey Gooseys), try dropping down to a 2.5mm (B/1 or C/2) hook. If your circle is smaller than mine (yes you, Tight Hookers), try using a 3.5mm (E/4) hook.

For the creatures, aim for an even, firm-but-not-strangled tension (à la amigurumi). Again, feel free to experiment with hook sizes if you are struggling with the stitches.

ERRATA AND PATTERN SUPPORT
Despite best efforts, gremlins do occasionally make their way into patterns.

Check **www.ponymctate.com** for errata and pattern support. If you need assistance with a pattern, you can get in touch with me there.

WHAT YOU CAN MAKE.

BIG SQUARE THINGS.

BLANKET
This book is designed to make a blanket measuring around 70cm x 82cm (27½in x 32¼in). That makes it roughly stroller size. Set up your squares like this:

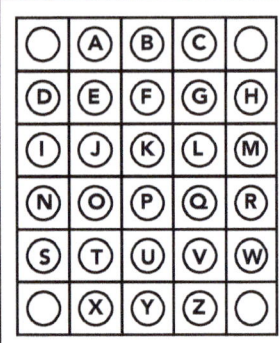

WALL HANGING
Or you could display your blanket on the wall instead. As a wall hanging, it is about A2 size. It is up to you whether you attach the fabric backing to the squares, or not. Hang the completed blanket from a length of dowelling rod or alternatively affix it straight to the wall.

BED RUNNER
The same 30 squares can be put together in a different way to make a bed runner, measuring 130cm x 46cm (51in x 18in). This is about the size for a double bed, or a single bed with overhang.

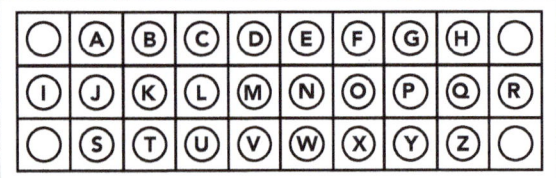

MAKING A BIGGER BLANKET?
If you want to make a bigger blanket, you could try:
- Interspersing extra background squares between the creature squares;
- Adding extra rounds to the background squares;
- Working a wider border.

A bigger blanket goes beyond the scope of this book, so do take the time to plan it out to make sure you have enough yarn.

OTHER IDEAS.

USING THE SQUARES
You can turn your A-B-Sea squares into other fun projects too. How about a cushion of your favourite squares? Or a tote bag? Or a framed line-up of letters spelling out a name? Or a mini wall hanging? Or bunting? Make bunting! That'd be super cool.

USING THE CREATURES
The creatures lend themselves to all kinds of creative embellishments. Stitch a safety pin onto the back and turn one into a unique brooch (see *Finishing Off* on page 73). Or sew them onto your favourite denim for a fresh new look. They make great patches on T-shirts and bags. Or fridge magnets? Gift tags? Go wild.

TECHNIQUES.

MAGIC LOOP.

A magic loop starts most of the circular shapes. This technique can be a little fiddly if you are unfamiliar with it but be patient. It creates a wonderfully tight first round without any gaps.

1. To begin, make a loop with the yarn. Leave a tail at the start about 10cm long and make sure it sits under the working end of the yarn. Insert your hook into this loop.
2. Pull the working end of the yarn through the loop.
3. Make a turning ch for the sts you will be working (the pattern will advise). Here I'm working a ch-1 for a rnd of dc.
4. Insert your hook back into the loop to work the first st.
5. Work the required number of sts into the loop. Catch both the loop and the tail end of the yarn around your sts.
6. Once the first rnd of sts is complete, pull the tail end of the yarn to (magically!) tighten the loop.

The pattern will advise whether you close the rnd with a sl st or keep going in a continuous spiral.

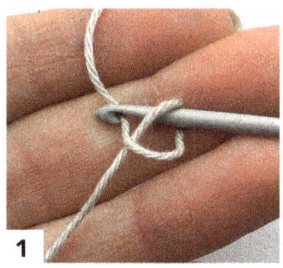 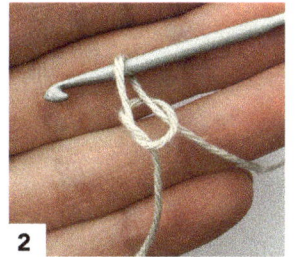
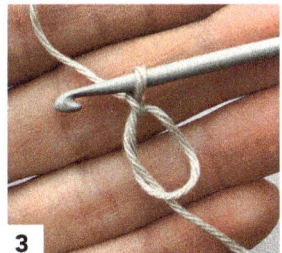 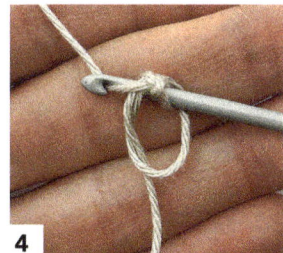

RNDS: WORK NEATER SEAMS.

Rnds 1–7 of the background squares are joined with a sl st but in a slightly different way than you might be used to. It makes for a neater seam and avoids the gaps and that obvious line of little parallel bars you usually get. But don't worry, it's not hard.

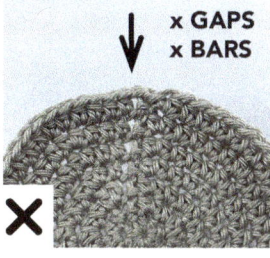 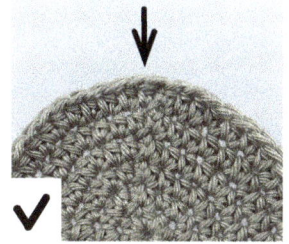

NORMAL SEAM
Last st in previous last st; sl st in initial ch to join.

NEATER SEAM
Last st in previous sl st; sl st in first st to join.

HOW TO WORK A NEATER SEAM

The pattern for Rnds 1–7 of the background squares calls for an increase as the final st of each rnd. Instead of working your 2sts in the last st of the previous rnd:

1. Work one st only in the last st of the previous rnd.
2. Work the second st of the increase into the sl st that joined the previous rnd.
3. Then skip the initial ch and sl st into the top of the first st to join the rnd.

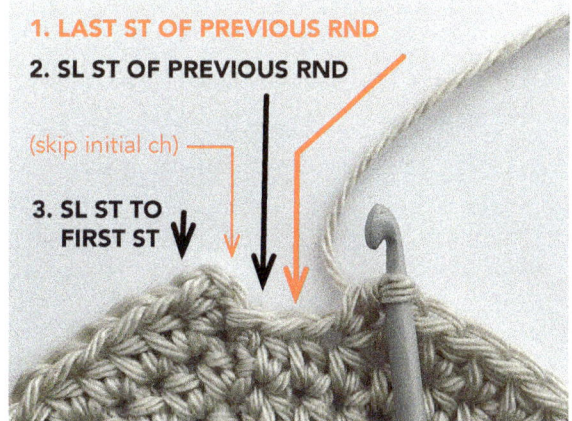

Fear not: the pattern makes it clear where you need to be working these sts.

BACK LOOPS/FRONT LOOPS.

Pay close attention to the anatomy of your sts. Each st has a back loop and a front loop. To work out which loop is which, hold your work upright at about nose level.

Look at the top of the line of sts you have just worked.

- The **back loop** is the side of the st away from you.
- The **front loop** is the side of the st that is closest to you.

Note that this will be the case regardless what side you are working. That means, even if you turn your work, the back loop will always be the loop furtherest away from you. I kid you not, it took me two years to work this out.

FASTEN OFF: INVISIBLE JOIN.

A clever way to fasten off rnds is by working an invisible join with a tapestry needle. It looks just like a st so you can't tell where the rnd has been joined. After the last st of the rnd, cut yarn leaving a 10cm tail and pull it up through the loops.

1. Thread yarn tail onto your tapestry needle. Skip the first st of the rnd and pass the needle under both loops of the second st, from RS to WS.
2. Then pass your needle under the BLO of the last st of the rnd, from RS to WS. Pull gently until the invisible join matches the other sts. Weave in end to secure the st.

 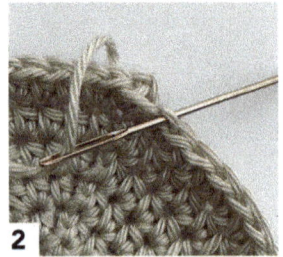

DECREASING: DC2TOG.

Most of the creatures are worked in turned rows. When decreasing, you will need to keep an eye on where the RS of your creature is. The loops you need to work into will change depending what side you are working on. All decreases in this book are worked in dc (pattern will say "dc2tog"). To work a decrease:

1. Insert your hook under the RS loops only of the next two stitches (it may be the BLO or the FLO; the pattern will advise).
2. Yarn over and draw through first two loops on your hook, just like a normal dc.
3. Finish off st in the usual way. Ta da! One dc2tog.
4. The decreased st from the WS.

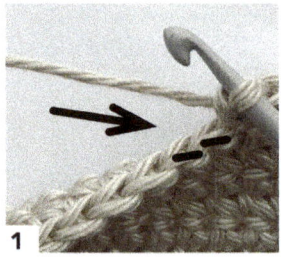 
 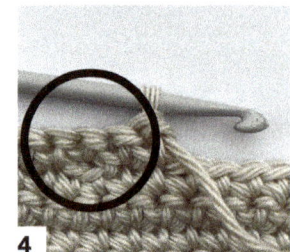

WEAVING IN ENDS.

For a project with this many ends to weave in, it pays to do it right. Here is a neat and sturdy method that won't undo over time.

1. If necessary, pull end through to WS. Using a tapestry needle, weave end under the legs of 3-4 sts. Check RS to make sure the woven end isn't visible on the front.
2. Skip the leg nearest your needle and weave the end back under the same sts. Cut yarn.

CHANGING COLOUR.

METHOD 1: STARTING WITH A NEW COLOUR
Pattern will say "Using (new colour), join yarn to..."

Use this method when you:
- have fastened off the previous colour; or
- are starting a new section (like a fin) by working into the ends of rows.

It's like joining yarn with a sl st but it avoids the bulky slip knot at the start. Join a new colour by simply pulling up a loop in the specified st. The pattern will advise you how many chs you then need to work to begin the rnd/row. Give the tail end a good tug and weave it in securely.

METHOD 2: MID-ROW
Pattern will say "Change to (new colour)..."

Use this method when you:
- need to change colour in the middle of a row; or
- are working stripes where you will need to pick up the old colour again.

To work this method, you begin the colour change the st before you want the new colour to start, i.e. at the last st of the old colour. Begin working the st with the old colour but use the new colour to work the last yarn over, finishing the st in the usual way. You will now be working with the new colour.

Read the pattern to see what to do with the old colour : in some cases you will drop it, ready to be picked up again on the next row. In other cases, you will carry the unused yarn along the row, working your sts around it and switching colours as required.

FRENCH KNOTS.

For the eyes and body decoration on the creatures, you work French knots. Here's how:

1. Bring your needle up to the RS and pass it under the leg of a nearby st. Make sure the yarn has a bit of slack between the crochet surface and the eye of the needle; you'll need it for the next step.
2. Wrap the yarn 3 times around the shaft of the needle.
3. Pull the needle through the wraps to tighten the knot.
4. Insert your needle back through to the WS and fasten off.

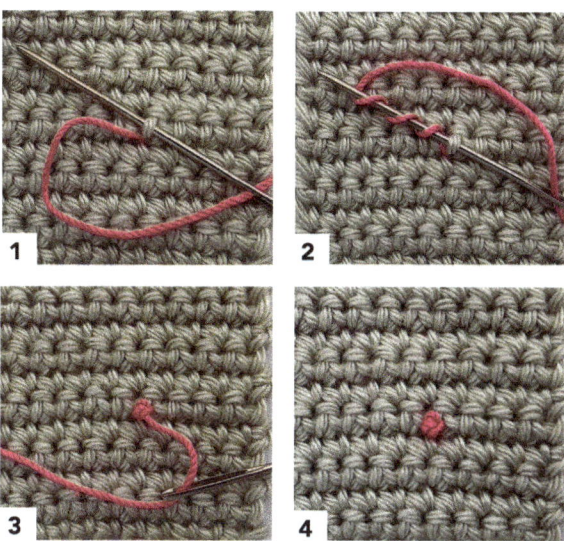

(French knots not your thing? Don't worry — you could work 3-4 little sts over the same place instead).

FINISHING OFF?
Remember, you'll find notes about:
- blocking,
- sewing down creatures,
- attaching the fabric backing,
- joining squares,
- the border; and
- using your creatures for other things

from page 68 onwards.

TECHNIQUES.

The Patterns.

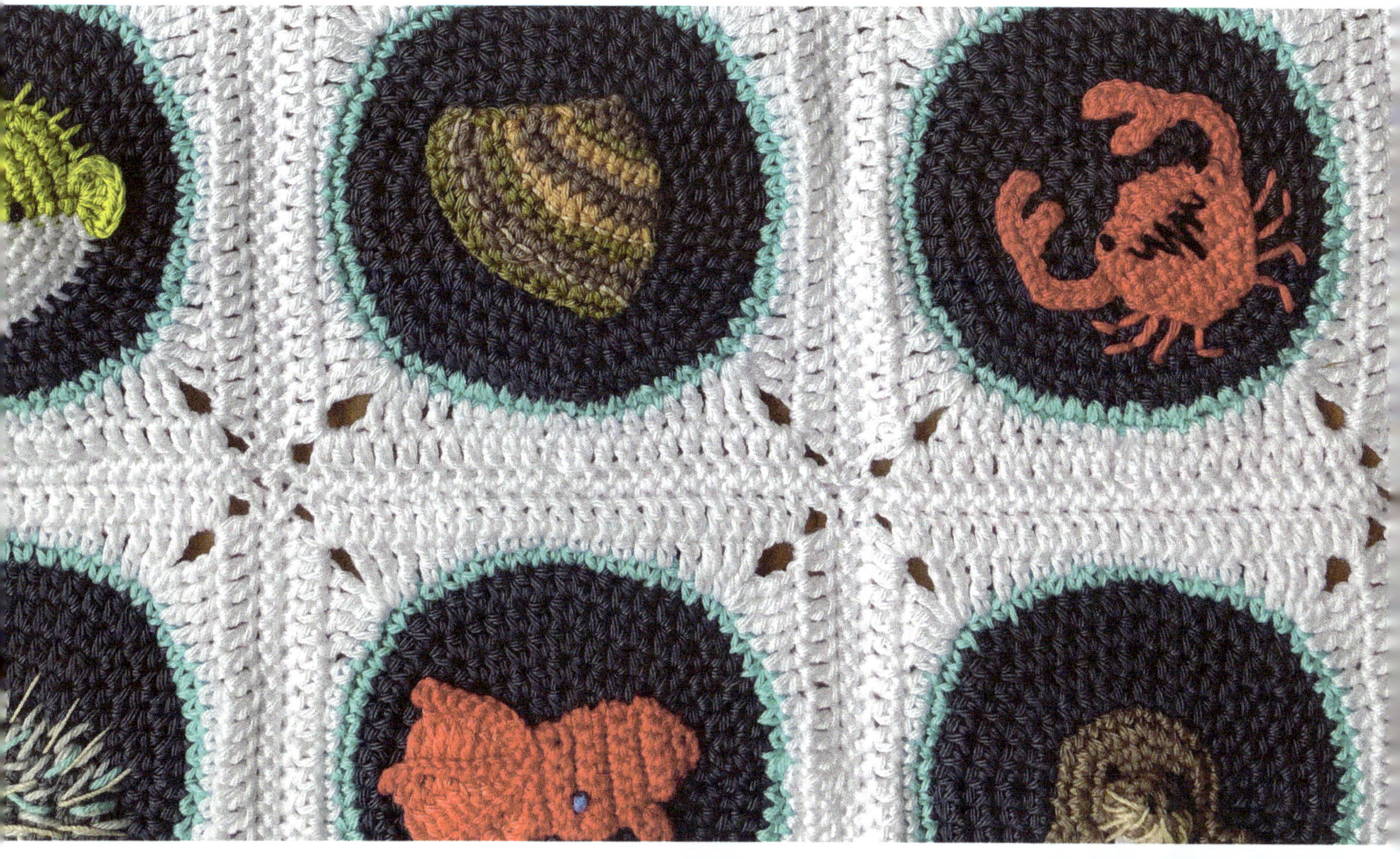

BACKGROUND SQUARE.

YARN.
Scheepjes Catona
393 (Charcoal)   253 (Tropic)
106 (Snow White)

NOTES.
- Make 26 background squares and 4 corner squares.
- The ch at the start of each rnd does not count as a st. Work the first st into the st at the base of this ch.
- When joining rnds, skip the ch and work the sl st into the first st of the rnd.
- Remember that on Rnds 2-7 the last htr is worked into the sl st of the previous rnd.
- See *Techniques* on page 11 for more information.

PATTERN.

Using **393 (Charcoal)**, make a magic loop.

Rnd 1 Ch2 (does not count as a st throughout), 8htr into the loop. Sl st to first st to join. [8 sts]
Rnd 2 Ch2, (2htr in each st) 7 times, htr in last st, htr in sl st of previous rnd. Sl st to join. [16 sts]
Rnd 3 Ch2, (htr in first st, 2htr in next st) 7 times, htr in last 2 sts, htr in sl st of previous rnd. Sl st to join. [24 sts]
Rnd 4 Ch2, (htr in first 2 sts, 2htr in next st) 7 times, htr in last 3 sts, htr in sl st of previous rnd. Sl st to join. [32 sts]
Rnd 5 Ch2, (htr in first 3 sts, 2htr in next st) 7 times, htr in last 4 sts, htr in sl st of previous rnd. Sl st to join. [40 sts]
Rnd 6 Ch2, (htr in first 4 sts, 2htr in next st) 7 times, htr in last 5 sts, htr in sl st of previous rnd. Sl st to join. [48 sts]
Rnd 7 Ch2, (htr in first 5 sts, 2htr in next st), htr in last 6 sts, htr in sl st of previous rnd. [56 sts]

Cut yarn and fasten off with an invisible join (see *Techniques* on page 12).

To prevent your inner circle growing corners, on the next rnd the location of the increases is staggered from the previous rnd. It means you start this rnd in the middle of what will become the side of the square (likewise for the two white rnds that follow).

Using **253 (Tropic)**, join yarn to the invisible join st (see *Techniques* on page 5).

Rnd 8 Ch1 (does not count as a st), dc in first 3 sts, 2dc in next st, (dc in next 6 sts, 2dc in next st) 7 times, dc in last 3 sts. [64 sts]

Cut yarn and fasten off with an invisible join. Using **106 (Snow White)**, join yarn to the invisible join st.

Rnd 9 Ch1 (does not count as a st), * dc in first 3 sts, htr in next 3 sts, tr in next st, dtr in next st, (2dtr, ch3, 2dtr) in next st, dtr in next st, tr in next st, htr in next 3 sts, dc in next 2 sts; repeat from * 3 more times to end. Sl st to first st join. [76 sts, 4 ch-3 sps // 19 sts per side]
Rnd 10 Ch3 (does not count as a st), * tr in each st to ch-3 sp, (2tr, 3ch, 2tr) in ch-3 sp; repeat from * 3 more times, tr in last 9 sts to end. [92 sts, 4 ch-3 sps // 23 sts per side]

Cut yarn, fasten off with an invisible join and weave in all ends. Block to measurements (see *Finishing Off* on page 68).

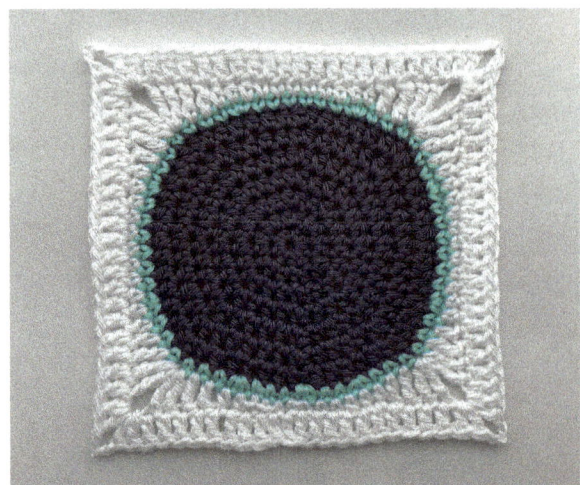

CORNER SQUARE.

As well as the 26 background squares, make 4 corner squares. The pattern is the same but alternate the colours:

- Rnds 1-7: **253 (Tropic)**
- Rnd 8: **393 (Charcoal)**
- Rnds 9-10: **106 (Snow White)**

ANEMONE.

YARN.

Scheepjes Catona
516 (Candy Apple)   280 (Lemon)
106 (Snow White)   518 (Marshmallow)

NOTES.
- Change colour in the last yarn over of the previous st: see *Techniques* on page 13.
- This is one of the trickier creatures, with a LOT of ends to weave in (sorry).
- Don't worry if your tentacles end up splaying all over the place. You can stitch them down when you sew your anemone onto its background square. Leave the ends free though; it will give your anemone a nice ruffly texture.

PATTERN.

BODY
Using **516 (Candy Apple)**, ch13.

Row 1 (RS) Dc in second ch from hook and in each ch to end. Turn. [12 sts]
Row 2 (WS) Ch1 (does not count as a st throughout), BLO dc2tog, dc in next 8 sts, BLO dc2tog. Turn. [10 sts]
Row 3 Ch1, dc in each st to end. Turn. [10 sts]
Row 4 Ch1, BLO dc2tog, dc in next 6 sts, BLO dc2tog. Turn. [8 sts]

Change to **280 (Lemon)**.
Row 5 Ch1, BLO dc in each st to end. Turn. [8 sts]
Row 6 Ch3, working into FLO, dc in st at base of ch and each st to end, ch3. Sl st into first st of Row 5. [8 sts + 2 ch-3 sps]

Fasten off.

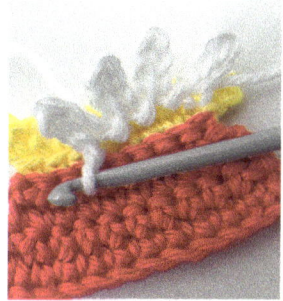

TENTACLES
Using **106 (Snow White)**, join yarn in unworked loop of first st on Row 5.

Row 7 (RS) (Ch4, sl st in second ch from hook and in each ch to end, sl st into unworked loops of next 2 sts of previous row) 11 times. At the side chs work into each ch rather than into the ch-sp, then turn to work into both loops of Row 6. Sl st into st at base of initial (white) ch-4. [11 tentacles]

Fasten off. Using **518 (Marshmallow)**, join yarn at top st of any tentacle. Ch 6, sl st in second ch from hook and in next 5 chs. Sl st into (white) st at base of (pink) ch.

Fasten off, cut yarn. Repeat for each tentacle. Weave in all ends and sew your anemone onto its background square (see *Finishing Off* on page 68).

BLOBFISH.

YARN.
Scheepjes Catona
408 (Old Rose)   518 (Marshmallow)
Scheepjes Maxi Sweet Treat
110 (Black)

NOTES.
- The BLO sts on Row 6 of the body leave unworked loops so you can work the nose up from them later.
- Avoid corners by working the last body row with no turning ch and sl st decreases.
- Once the body is complete, the fins are worked into the row edges.

PATTERN.

BODY
Using **408 (Old Rose)**, ch18.

Row 1 (RS) Dc in second ch from hook and in each ch to end. Turn. [17 sts]
Row 2 (WS) Ch1 (does not count as a st throughout), dc in each st to end. Turn. [17 sts]
Row 3 Ch1, FLO dc2tog, dc in next 13 sts, FLO dc2tog. Turn. [15 sts]
Row 4 Ch1, dc in each st to end. Turn. [15 sts]
Row 5 Ch1, FLO dc2tog, dc in next 11 sts, FLO dc2tog. Turn. [13 sts]
Row 6 Ch1, BLO dc2tog, dc in next 2 sts, FLO dc in next 5 sts, dc in next 2 sts, BLO dc2tog. Turn. [11 sts]
Row 7 Ch1, FLO dc2tog, dc in next 7 sts, FLO dc2tog. Turn. [9 sts]
Row 8 Ch1, BLO dc2tog, dc in next 5 sts, BLO dc2tog. Turn. [7 sts]

Row 9 Without working a turning ch, FLO slst2tog, dc in next 3 sts, FLO slst2tog. [5 sts]

Fasten off.

NOSE
The nose is worked into the unworked loops from Row 6. Rotate the body 180° so the foundation ch is uppermost. Insert your hook in the first loop, from bottom to top. Using **Old Rose**, join yarn and ch1.

Row 1 (RS) Dc in first st, htr in next st, tr in next st, htr in next st, dc in last st. [5 sts]

Fasten off.

BLOBFISH. 18

MOUTH
Using **518 (Marshmallow)**, ch9.

Row 1 (RS) 2dc in second ch from hook, dc in next 6 chs, 2dc in last ch. [10 sts]

Fasten off, leaving a 20cm tail. Using a tapestry needle, sew mouth onto the body. Tuck it under the nose and arrange it so the ends of the mouth turn down. Weave in ends.

> **WHAT IS A BLOBFISH?**
> This mysterious fish dwells at great depths off the coast of Australia and New Zealand. It has no teeth or bones and very little muscle mass so it can't self-propel. To eat, it floats above the sea floor with its mouths open and waits for food to drop by. Scientists think blobfish probably look less blobby in their natural deep sea habitat. Decompression damage caused when they are brought to the surface of the ocean is likely to account for their deflated appearance.

PECTORAL FINS
Using **Marshmallow**, join yarn to body at last st of Row 2. Ch2.

Row 1 (RS) In the same st (htr, 2tr, htr), ch2, sl st into same st. Fasten off.

Repeat Row 1 for the other fin, working in first st of Body Row 2.

EYES
Using **Maxi Sweet Treat 110 (Black)** and a tapestry needle, work a French knot for each eye (see *Techniques* on page 13). Place the eyes one row up and one stitch out from either side of the top of the nose. Use the main photo as a guide.

Weave in all ends. Sew your blobfish onto its background square (see *Finishing Off* on page 68).

BLOBFISH.

CLOWNFISH.

YARN.
⭐⭐⭐

Scheepjes Catona
281 (Tangerine)   106 (Snow White)
Scheepjes Maxi Sweet Treat
110 (Black)

NOTES.
- The BLO sts in the middle of the body leave unworked loops so you can work the pectoral fin up from them later.
- Change colour in the last yarn over of the previous st: see *Techniques* on page 13.
- Where possible, yarn is uncut between stripes to reduce the number of ends to sew in. The pattern will tell you when to cut your yarn.

PATTERN.

BODY
Using **281 (Tangerine)**, ch2.

Row 1 (WS) 2dc in second ch from hook. Turn. [2 sts]
Row 2 (RS) Ch1 (does not count as a st throughout), 2dc in each st to end. Turn. [4 sts]
Row 3 Ch1, 2dc in first st, dc in next 2 sts, 2dc in last st. Turn. [6 sts]
Row 4 Ch1, 2dc in first st, dc in next 4 sts, 2dc in last st. Turn. [8 sts]

Change to **106 (Snow White)**. Do not cut Tangerine.
Row 5 Ch1, dc in each st to end. Turn. [8 sts]
Row 6 Repeat Row 5. Turn. [8 sts]

Change to **Tangerine**. Cut Snow White.
Row 7 Ch1, dc in next 3 sts, FLO dc in next 3 sts, dc in last 2 sts. Turn. [8 sts]
Rows 8-9 Repeat Row 5. [8 sts]

Change to **Snow White**. Do not cut Tangerine.
Rows 10-11 Repeat Row 5. [8 sts]

Change to **Tangerine**. Do not cut Snow White.
Row 12 Ch1, FLO dc2tog, dc in each st to end. Turn. [7 sts]
Row 13 Ch1, BLO dc2tog, dc in each st to end. Turn. [6 sts].

Change to **Snow White**. Do not cut Tangerine.
Row 14 Repeat Row 12. [5 sts]
Row 15 Ch1, BLO dc2tog, dc in next st, BLO dc2tog. Turn. [3 sts]

Change to **Tangerine** for tail. Cut Snow White.

BODY

TAIL

TAIL
The tail continues on from Row 15 of the body.

Row 1 (RS) Ch3, 2tr in each st to end, ch3, sl st in same st as last 2-tr group. Fasten off.

CLOWNFISH.

FINS

The fins are worked along the edges of the body, inserting your hook into the ends of rows. Treat each row end as one st.

SOFT DORSAL FIN
(THE BACK ONE ON TOP)
Using **Tangerine**, join yarn to body in the end of Row 13. Ch1.

Row 1 (RS) Dc in st at base of ch, htr in the next st, ch2, sl st into same st as htr. Fasten off.

SPINY DORSAL FIN
(THE FRONT ONE ON TOP)
Using **Tangerine**, join yarn to body in the end of Row 9. Ch1.

Row 1 (RS) Dc in st at base of ch, htr in next st, tr in next st, ch3, sl st into same st as tr. Fasten off.

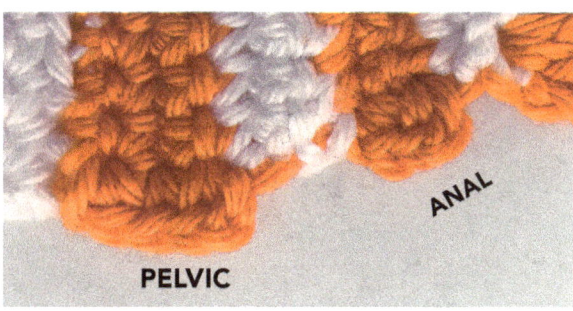

PELVIC FIN
(THE FRONT ONE UNDERNEATH)
Using **Tangerine**, join yarn to body in the end of Row 8. Ch 1.

Row 1 (RS) Dc in st at base of ch and next 2 sts, sl st into same st as dc. Fasten off.

ANAL FIN
(THE BACK ONE UNDERNEATH)
Repeat as for pelvic fin, joining yarn to body in the end of Row 12 and working dc in st at base of ch and next st.

PECTORAL FIN
(THE ONE ON THE SIDE)
Using **Tangerine**, join yarn to lower-most unworked loop on Row 7. Ch3.

Row 1 (RS) Tr in st at base of ch and in each st to end, ch 3, sl st into same st as last tr. Fasten off.

FIN TRIM — ALL FINS AND TAIL
Using **Maxi Sweet Treat 110 (Black)**, join yarn to first st of fin. Ch1.

Row 1 (RS) Dc in st at base of ch and in each st to end. Fasten off.

Repeat for other fins and tail.

BLACK LINES
Using **Maxi Sweet Treat Black** and a tapestry needle, embroider a line along each side of the white stripes. Use the main photo as a guide. Fasten off.

EYE
Using **Maxi Sweet Treat Black** and a tapestry needle, work a French knot for the eye (see *Techniques* on page 13). Place it on Row 3 between the third and fourth sts, using the main photo as a guide.

Weave in all ends. Sew your clownfish onto its background square (see *Finishing Off* on page 68).

DEEP SEA ANGLER.

YARN.

Scheepjes Catona
- 507 (Chocolate)
- 280 (Lemon)
- 254 (Moon Rock)
- 106 (Snow White)

Scheepjes Maxi Sweet Treat
- 110 (Black)

NOTES.
- The BLO sts in the middle of the body leave an unworked loop so you can work the pectoral up from it later.
- The teeth are embroidered on once you've sewn your deep sea angler onto its background square.
- Leave the rod and lure on its head free to dangle.

PATTERN.

BODY
Using **507 (Chocolate)**, ch3.

Row 1 (RS) Dc in second ch from the hook and next ch. Turn. [2 sts]
Row 2 (WS) Ch1 (does not count as a st throughout), 2dc in each st to end. Turn. [4 sts]
Row 3 Ch1, 2dc in first st, dc in each st until 1 st remains, 2dc in last st. Turn. [6 sts]
Row 4 Ch1, dc in each st to end. Turn. [6 sts]
Row 5 Repeat Row 3. Turn. [8 sts]
Row 6 Ch1, dc in first 2 sts, FLO dc, dc in each st to end. Turn. [8 sts]
Row 7 Repeat Row 3. Turn. [10 sts]
Row 8 Repeat Row 4. Turn. [10 sts]
Row 9 Ch1, dc in first 7 sts, htr in next st, tr in next st, dtr in last st. [10 sts]

Fasten off.

LOWER JAW
Using **Chocolate**, join yarn in first st of Row 9. Ch9.

Row 1 (RS) Dc in second ch from hook, skip next ch, dc in next 4 chs, skip next ch, dc in next st on body. [6 sts]

Fasten off.

ROD AND LURE (THE DANGLY BIT)

Rod Using **Chocolate**, join yarn to end of Row 7. Ch12. Fasten off.

Lure Using **280 (Lemon)**, make a magic loop.

Rnd 1 Ch1, 6dc into the loop, sl st to close. [6 sts]

Fasten off, using the yarn tail to sew the lure onto the rod with a couple of stitches.

LIPS
Using **254 (Moon Rock)**, join yarn in end st of lower jaw and sl st in each st around mouth. Use the main picture as a guide. Fasten off.

TAIL
Using **Moon Rock**, join yarn to first ch of body foundation ch. Ch3.

Row 1 (RS) Tr in st at base of ch, tr in next st, ch 3, sl st to same st as last tr.

Fasten off.

TEETH
The teeth are embroidered on after you've sewn your deep sea angler onto its background square (see *Finishing Off* on page 68).

With **Catona 106 (Snow White)** and a tapestry needle, sew about 12 stitches around the mouth, anchoring them in the edge of the mouth. Use shorter stitches in the corner of the mouth and longer stitches towards the ends, using the main photo as a guide.

Weave in ends.

> **WHAT IS THE ROD AND LURE FOR?**
> The deep sea angler lives in the darkest depths of the sea, where no sunlight can penetrate. To attract prey, this fish lights up the fleshy growth protruding from its head by way of bioluminescence. When something tasty swims up to investigate... chomp.

PECTORAL FIN
Using **Moon Rock**, join yarn to body at unworked loop on Row 6. Ch2.

Row 1 (RS) 2htr in st at base of ch, ch2, sl st to same st.

Fasten off and weave in all ends.

EYE
Using **Maxi Sweet Treat 110 (Black)** and a tapestry needle, work a French knot for the eye (see *Techniques* on page 13). Place it on Row 9 between the seventh and eighth sts, using the main photo as a guide.

DEEP SEA ANGLER.

ELECTRIC EEL.

YARN.
Scheepjes Catona
395 (Willow)
254 (Moon Rock)
208 (Yellow Gold)
Scheepjes Maxi Sweet Treat
110 (Black)

NOTES.
- The fin is worked into the unworked side of the foundation ch.
- The lightening bolt "zaps" are embroidered on once you've sewn your electric eel onto its background square.

PATTERN.

BODY
Using **395 (Willow)**, ch29.

Row 1 (RS) Sl st in second ch from the hook and next st, dc in next st, htr in next st, then tr in each st until 2 sts remain, htr in next st, dc in last st. [28 sts]

Fasten off and weave in ends, giving the head a rounded point.

FIN
The fin is worked along the lower-side of the body, along the unworked side of the foundation ch.

Using **254 (Moon Rock)**, join yarn at the fifth ch of the foundation ch (counting from the head).

Row 1 (RS) Dc in next st and in each st to end, sl st in turning ch of previous row and fasten off. [24 sts]

EYE
Using **Maxi Sweet Treat 110 (Black)** and a tapestry needle, work a French knot for the eye (see *Techniques* on page 13). Place it on the second st along on the head, using the main photo as a guide. Weave in ends.

ARRANGING YOUR EEL
When sewing your eel onto its background square, fold it into a Z-shape. Use the main photo as a guide. Leave enough space around the tail for the lightning bolt zaps.

LIGHTNING BOLT ZAPS
The zaps are embroidered on after you've sewn your electric eel onto its background square (see *Finishing Off* on page 68).

Using **Catona 208 (Yellow Gold)** and a tapestry needle, sew 5 zaps near the end of the tail using the main photo as a guide. Each zap takes 3 stitches.

Weave in all ends.

FLYING FISH.

YARN.

Scheepjes Catona
511 (Cornflower)   172 (Pale Silver)
Scheepjes Maxi Sweet Treat
074 (Mercury)   110 (Black)

NOTES.
- The body and tail are worked in one piece.
- Once the body is complete, the fins are worked into the row edges. Treat each row end as one st.
- The pectoral fins (the wings) are worked separately and sewn on to the completed body, before sewing your flying fish onto its background square.

PATTERN.

BODY
Using **172 (Pale Silver)**, ch4.

Row 1 (RS) 3tr in fourth ch from hook. Turn. [3 sts]
Row 2 (WS) Ch1 (does not count as a st throughout), dc in each st until 1 st remains, 2dc in last st. Turn. [4 sts]
Row 3 Ch1, dc in each st to end. Turn. [4 sts]

Change to **511 (Cornflower)**. Cut Pale Silver.
Row 4 Ch1, dc in each st until 1 st remains, 2dc in last st. Turn. [5 sts]
Row 5 Repeat Row 3. [5 sts]
Row 6 Ch1, dc in each st until 2 sts remain, htr in next st, tr in last st. Turn. [5 sts]
Row 7 Ch3, tr in first st, htr in next st, dc in each st to end. Turn. [5 sts]
Rows 8-9 Repeat Row 3. Turn. [5 sts]
Row 10 Ch1, dc in first 2 sts, FLO dc2tog, dc. Turn. [4 sts]
Row 11 Repeat Row 3. [4 sts]
Row 12 Repeat Row 10. [3 sts]
Row 13 Ch1, BLO dc2tog, dc in last st. Turn. [2 sts]

Leave loop on hook for tail.

TAIL
Ch 5, sl st in second ch from hook and in next ch, dc in next 2 chs, dc to body in last st of Row 13; ch5, sl st in second ch from hook and in next ch, dc in next 2 chs, sl st to body in first st of Row 13. Fasten off.

**DORSAL FIN
(THE LITTLE ONE ON TOP)**
Using **Pale Silver**, join yarn to body at end of Row 12.

Row 1 Ch1, dc in first st and in next st along. Fasten off.

**PELVIC FIN
(THE BIG ONE UNDERNEATH)**
Using **Pale Silver**, join yarn to body at end of Row 12.

Row 1 Ch3, (tr, 2dtr) in st at base of ch. Fasten off.

**PECTORAL FINS — MAKE 2 THE SAME
(THE WINGS)**
The pectoral fins are worked separately then sewn onto the body. Using **Pale Silver**, ch13.

Row 1 Sl st in first 2 chs, dc in next 2 chs, htr in next 2 chs, tr in next 2 chs, dtr in next 2 chs, ch3, sl st to same st as last dtr — 2 chs unworked. [10 sts]

Fasten off, leaving a 10cm tail for sewing.

Sew pectoral fins to the body, arranging one of the wings to sit behind the body. Use the photo here and the main photo as a guide.

SCALES
Using **Maxi Sweet Treat 074 (Mercury)** and a tapestry needle, work around 10 cross stitches across the top half of the body for scales.

Weave in ends.

EYE
Using **Maxi Sweet Treat 110 (Black)** and a tapestry needle, work a French knot for the eye (see *Techniques* on page 13). Place it on Row 1 between the second and third sts, using the main photo as a guide.

Weave in all ends. Sew your flying fish onto its background square (see *Finishing Off* on page 68).

HOW DO FLYING FISH FLY?
Flying fish can propel themselves at speed out of the water, then glide on their large wing-like pectoral fins for considerable distances. They do so to evade predators. Typically, they can fly for around 50m (160 ft) at speeds of more than 70 km/h (43mph), beating their tail against the surface of the water for consecutive glides.

GREAT WHITE SHARK.

YARN.

Scheepjes Catona
    106 (Snow White)   110 (Black)
    172 (Pale Silver)
Scheepjes Maxi Sweet Treat
    238 (Powder Pink)   110 (Black)

NOTES.
- The body starts with a magic loop but is then worked in turned rows.
- The lower edge of the body is designed to curve to match the background square.
- The teeth and gums are embroidered on once the body is complete and before you sew your great white shark onto its background square.

PATTERN.

BODY
Using **106 (Snow White)**, make a magic loop.

Row 1 (WS) Ch1 (does not count as a st throughout), 6dc into the loop. Do not join. Turn. [6 sts]

Row 2 (RS) Ch1, (2dc in same st, dc) 3 times. Turn. [9 sts]

Row 3 Ch1, (2dc in same st, dc in next 2 sts) 3 times. Turn. [12 sts]

Row 4 Ch1, dc in first st, skip next st, dc in next 2 sts, htr, 2tr in next 2 sts, htr, dc in next 2 sts, skip st, dc in last st. Turn. [12 sts]

Row 5 Ch1, dc in first 4 sts, 2htr in next st, 2tr in next 2 sts, 2htr in next st, dc in last 4 sts. Turn. [16 sts]

Remove loop from hook. You will need to pick it back up again at Row 9.

Using **110 (Black)** and with WS facing, join yarn to body in third st from end.

Row 6 (RS) Ch1, dc in first 3 sts, 2dc in next st, htr in next st, 2tr in next 2 sts, htr in next st, 2dc in next st, dc in next 3 sts. Turn. [16 sts]

Row 7 (WS) Do not work turning ch, skip first st, sl st, dc in next 3 sts, 2dc in next st, htr in next st, 2tr in next 2 sts, htr in next st, 2dc in next st, dc in next 3 sts, skip st, sl st in last st. [18 sts]

Cut **Black** and pick up **Snow White** again by sliding hook into working loop left after Row 5, RS facing.

Row 8 (RS) Ch2, htr in first 2 (white) sts, dc in next 6 (black) sts, 2dc in next st, htr, 2tr in next 2 sts, htr, 2dc in next st, dc in next 6 (black) sts, htr in last 2 (white) sts. Turn. [26 sts]

Cut **Snow White**.

The next row is a short row, which means the yarn is rejoined a few stitches in and at the end of the row a few stitches are left unworked. It creates a nice, sharp pointy nose. With WS facing, rejoin **Snow White** in ninth st from end.

Row 9 (WS) Ch1, dc in next 3 sts, htr, 2tr in next 2 sts, htr, dc in next 3 sts. [12 sts]

Fasten off.

WS

Using **172 (Pale Silver)** and with RS facing, join yarn at first st of Row 8. Ch1.

Row 10 (RS) Dc in first 13 sts, (dc, tr) in next st, (tr, dc) in next st, dc in each st to end. [30 sts]

Fasten off and weave in ends.

TEETH
Using **Snow White** and a tapestry needle, add a row of stitches for teeth along the edges of the black area. Use the needle to pierce the crochet stitches, rather than working into the spaces between stitches. Refer to the photo above and the main photo as a guide.

GUMS
Using **Maxi Sweet Treat 238 (Powder Pink)** and a tapestry needle, embroider a line of stitches along Rows 5 and 8 around the mouth.

EYES
Using **Maxi Sweet Treat 110 (Black)** and a tapestry needle, work a French knot for each eye on Row 10 in the eighth stitches from each end (see *Techniques* on page 13). Place your knots in between the front and back loops. Use the main photo as a guide.

Weave in all ends. Sew your great white shark onto its background square (see *Finishing Off* on page 68).

> **DUUUUN DUN... DUUUUN DUN...**
> Great white sharks get a bit of a bad rap. *Jaws* didn't help (though the movie gave us a marvellously terrifying theme song). Great whites are indeed fearsome predators and yes, as a species they account for the majority of attacks on humans. But 80% of their victims survive — sharks will bite people but they rarely eat them. Biologists propose that they are giving humans a curious nibble rather than hunting them as a food source. And lest we forget, vending machines kill more people annually than great white sharks. Yes, vending machines.

HUMUHUMUNUKUNUKUAPUA'A.

YARN.

Scheepjes Catona
- 106 (Snow White)
- 208 (Yellow Gold)
- 280 (Lemon)
- 110 (Black)
- 397 (Cyan)

NOTES.
- This is one of the trickier creatures: there are several mid-row colour changes in a small area and lots of embroidery.
- Colour changes in the pattern are indicated with written instructions, as well as coloured text. See *Techniques* on page 13.
- Don't carry your unused yarn under your sts. Just drop it, ready to pick up again on the next row.

PATTERN.

BODY
Using **106 (Snow White)**, ch3.

Row 1 (RS) Dc in second ch from hook and in next ch. Turn. [2 sts]
Row 2 (WS) Ch1 (does not count as a st throughout), dc in each st to end. Turn. [2 sts]
Row 3 Ch1, 2dc in each st to end. Turn. [4 sts]
Row 4 Ch1, 2dc in first st, dc in next 2 sts, 2dc in last st. Turn. [6 sts]
Row 5 Ch1, 2dc first st, dc in each st to end. Turn. [7 sts]

Rows 6-18 use the following colours:
- **106 (Snow White)**....referred to as "White"
- **110 (Black)**.........................."Black"
- **208 (Yellow Gold)**..........................."Yellow"

Colour changes are indicated with written instructions, as well as coloured text.

Row 6 Ch1, dc in first 3 sts, (change to Black) dc in next 3 sts, 2dc in last st. Turn. [8 sts]
Row 7 Ch1, dc in first 6 sts, (change to White) dc in last 2 sts. Turn. [8 sts]
Row 8 Ch1, dc in first 2 sts, (change to Black) dc in next 6 sts, (change to Yellow). Turn. [8 sts]
Row 9 Ch1, dc in first 2 sts, (change to Black) dc in next 5 sts, (change to White) dc in last st. Turn. [8 sts]
Row 10 Ch1, dc in first st, (change to Black) dc in next 5 sts, (change to Yellow) dc in last 2 sts. Turn. [8 sts]
Row 11 Ch1, dc in first 3 sts, (change to Black) dc in next 4 sts, (change to White) dc in last st, (change to Black). Turn. [8 sts]

Cut White, leaving a 30cm tail.

Row 12 Ch1, dc in first 2 sts, BLO dc2tog, dc in next st, (change to Yellow) dc in next 3 sts. Turn. [7 sts]
Row 13 Ch1, dc in first 3 sts, (change to Black) dc in next 4 sts. Turn. [7 sts]
Row 14 Ch1, dc in first st, BLO dc2tog, dc in next st, (change to Yellow) dc in next 3 sts. Turn. [6 sts]
Row 15 Ch1, dc in first st, FLO dc2tog, (change to Black) dc in last 3 sts. Turn. [5 sts]
Row 16 Ch1, dc in first 2 sts, (change to Yellow) dc in last 3 sts. Turn. [5 sts]
Row 17 Ch1, dc in first st, FLO dc2tog, (change to Black), dc in last 2 sts. Turn. [4 sts]
Row 18 Ch1, BLO dc2tog, (change to Yellow) BLO dc2tog. [2 sts]

Change to **397 (Cyan)** for the tail, which continues from Row 18. Turn.

Cut Yellow and Black leaving 30cm yarn tails. You will use the tails later to "colour in" the untidy line of stitches left by the colour changes.

TAIL
Row 1 (RS) Ch3, 3tr in st at base of ch and in next st, ch3, sl st to same st as last 3tr-goup. Fasten off.

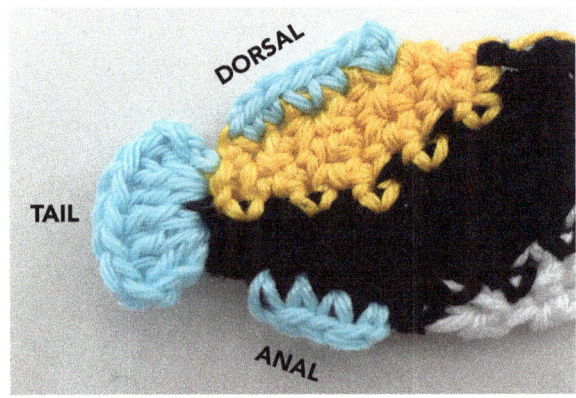

FINS
The fins are worked along the edges of the body, into the ends of rows. Treat each row end as a st.

DORSAL FIN (THE TOP ONE)
Using **Cyan**, join yarn to the body in the end of Row 12. Ch1.

Row 1 (RS) Dc in st at base of ch and in each of the next 5 sts. Fasten off.

ANAL FIN (THE BOTTOM ONE)
Using **Cyan**, join yarn to the body in the end of Row 16. Ch1.

Row 1 (RS) Skip st at base of ch, dc in next st and in each of the next 3 sts. Fasten off.

TIDY UP THE COLOUR-CHANGE EDGES
Using a tapestry needle and the leftover yarn tails from the body, cover up the colour changes with a series of small stitches.

Start with **Black**, stitching over the wayward Yellow and White stitches; then switch to the remaining colours of yarn to fill in gaps, if any. Fasten off.

FINE LINES
Use a tapestry needle to embroider fine lines onto the body, as set out below. Refer to the photos here and the main photo as a guide.

First, using **Yellow Gold**, embroider 3-4 long sts from the middle of Row 16 to below the tail. Aim to leave a small black triangle at the tail.

Second, using **Cyan**, embroider a line around the front of the Yellow section down to Row 13. Stitch a small vertical line near the end of the nose.

HUMUHUMUNUKUNUKUAPUA'A.

3

Third, using **280 (Lemon)**, embroider an outline around the small black triangle near the tail, and a larger V-shaped line from the two fins down to the Cyan line. Weave in all ends.

EYE

The eye of a humuhumunukunukuapua'a sits on the black part of its body. Since you won't be able to distinguish a black embroidered eye on a black background, just leave it off.

Sew your humuhumunukunukuapua'a onto its background square (see *Finishing Off* on page 68).

HUMU-WHAT?!
The humuhumunukunukuapua'a is a tropical reef trigger fish and is the state fish of Hawaii. Here's how you pronounce its awesome name:

hu-mu, hu-mu • nu-ku, nu-ku • a-pwah-a

INEXPLICABLE SHRIMPGOBY.

YARN.
Scheepjes Catona
  172 (Light Silver)
  106 (Snow White)
Scheepjes Maxi Sweet Treat
  074 (Mercury)
  110 (Black)

NOTES.
- Yarn is left uncut between stripes to reduce the number of ends to sew in.
- Once the body is complete, the fins are worked into the row edges.

PATTERN.

BODY
Using **172 (Pale Silver)**, ch2.

Row 1 (RS) 2dc in second ch from hook. Turn. [2 sts]
Row 2 (WS) Ch1 (does not count as a st throughout), 2dc in each st to end. Turn. [4 sts]
Row 3 Ch1, dc in next 3 sts, 2dc in last st. Turn. [5 sts]

Change to **106 (Snow White)**. Do not cut unused colour between rows until advised.
Row 4 2dc in first st, dc in next 5 sts to end. Turn. [6 sts]
Row 5 Ch1, dc in each st to end. [6 sts]

Change to **Pale Silver**.
Rows 6-7 Repeat Row 5. Turn. [6 sts]

Change to **Snow White**.
Row 8 Ch1, dc in first st, BLO dc2tog, dc in each st to end. Turn. [5 sts]
Row 9 Repeat Row 5. Turn. [5 sts]

Change to **Pale Silver**.
Rows 10-11 Repeat Row 5. Turn. [5 sts]

Change to **Snow White**.
Row 12 Ch1, dc in first st, BLO dc2tog, dc in last 2 sts. Turn. [4 sts]

Row 13 Repeat Row 5. [4 sts]

Change to **Pale Silver**.
Rows 14-15 Repeat Row 5. Turn. [4 sts]

Change to **Snow White**.
Row 16 Repeat Row 8. Turn. [3 sts]
Row 17 Repeat Row 5. Turn. [3 sts]

Change to **Pale Silver**. Cut Snow White.
Row 18 Ch1, BLO dc2tog, dc in last st. Turn. [2 sts]

Leave loop on hook for tail.

TAIL
The tail continues on from Row 18.

Row 1 Ch3, 3tr in each st to end, ch3, sl st to same st as last tr. Fasten off.

FINS

The fins are worked along the edges of the body into the ends of the body rows. Treat each row end as a st.

SOFT DORSAL FIN
(THE TOP ONE AT THE BACK)

Using **Pale Silver**, join yarn to the body in the end of Row 15. Ch2.

Row 1 (RS) Htr in st at base of ch, tr in each of next 4 sts. Fasten off.

SPINY DORSAL FIN
(THE TOP ONE AT THE FRONT)

Using **Pale Silver**, join yarn to the body in the end of Row 8. Ch3.

Row 1 (RS) Tr in st at base of ch, (tr, dtr) in next st. Fasten off.

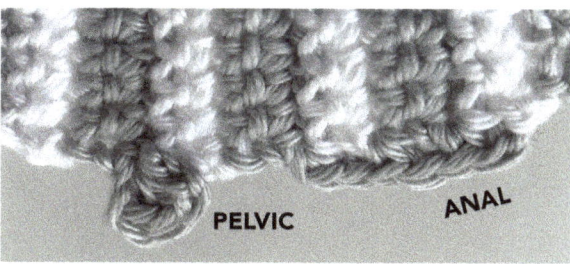

PELVIC FIN
(THE BOTTOM ONE AT THE FRONT)

Using **Pale Silver**, join yarn to the body in the end of Row 7. Ch2.

Row 1 (RS) 2htr in st at base of ch, ch2, sl st to same st. Fasten off.

ANAL FIN
(THE BOTTOM ONE AT THE BACK)

Using **Pale Silver**, join yarn to the body in the end of Row 11. Ch1.

Row 1 (RS) Dc in st at base of ch and the next 5 sts. Fasten off.

SPOTS

The spots are embroidered on once the body is complete.

Using **Maxi Sweet Treat 074 (Mercury)** and a tapestry needle, work around 10 French knots along the top half of the body (see *Techniques* on page 13).

Use the photo below and the main photo as a guide. Fasten off.

EYE

Using **Maxi Sweet Treat 110 (Black)** and a tapestry needle, work a French knot for the eye. Place it on Row 3 at the third st along, using the main photo as a guide.

Weave in all ends. Sew your inexplicable shrimpgoby onto its background square (see *Finishing Off* on page 68).

WHY SO INEXPLICABLE?
Good question. I had to consult the godfather of gobies, Dr Doug Hoese from Australia Museum, on this one. He very kindly explained that this fish was originally described as having odd teeth in the roof of its mouth. At the time, the function of the teeth was unknown. We now know that these "teeth" are actually a large bone, called a vomer. The vomer becomes apparent when the fish, stressed, inflates its mouth, pushing the bone down into its mouth. Preserving specimens in solution exaggerates the fake fangs. Inexplicable no more — thanks, Dr Hoese!

INEXPLICABLE SHRIMPGOBY.

JELLYFISH.

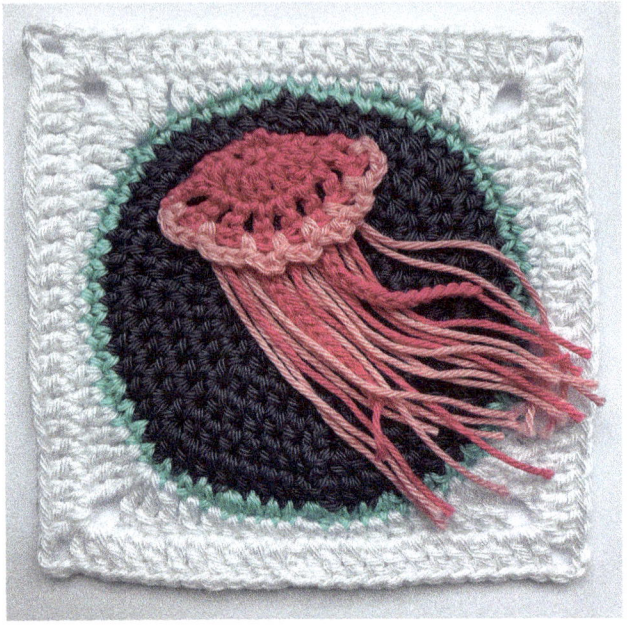

YARN.
Scheepjes Catona
114 (Shocking Pink)
518 (Marshmallow)

NOTES.
- This creature is worked in turned rows.
- The tentacles are knotted onto the lower row of crochet stitches. Leave them long and swishy (though see the warning below if a young child will be using the blanket.
- When complete, sew your jellyfish onto its background square (see *Finishing Off* on page 68).

PATTERN.

BELL (THE GLOOPY TOP BIT)
Using **114 (Shocking Pink)** and leaving a 10cm tail at the start, ch2.

Row 1 (WS) 4dc in second ch from the hook. Turn. [4 sts]
Row 2 (RS) Ch3, 2tr in st at base of ch and each st to end. Turn. [8 sts]
Row 3 Ch4 (counts as tr, ch), (tr, ch) in st at base of ch and each st until 1 st remains, tr in last st. Turn. [9 tr, 8 ch-sps]

Change to **518 (Marshmallow)**.

Row 4 Ch1, dc in ch1-sp, (ch3, skip tr, dc in next ch1-sp) 7 times. (8 sts, 7 ch-groups).

Fasten off and weave in ends, using foundation ch tail to stitch over hole from Row 1.

ORAL ARMS — MAKE 2 THE SAME (THE FAT TENTACLES)
Using **Shocking Pink** and with WS facing, join yarn to one of the middle tr of Row 3, leaving a 10cm tail at the start. Ch14. Fasten off and cut yarn to desired tentacle length. Secure starting tail by weaving it under 2-3 sts then trim to desired tentacle length.

TENTACLES (THE SKINNY ONES)
Using a mix of **Marshmallow** and **Shocking Pink**, cut 9 strands of yarn 20cm (9in) long. Double them over and knot them along Row 3. Trim ends to desired tentacle length.

WARNING
The knots attaching the tentacles can loosen over time, freeing the strands of yarn. This is a potential choking or inhalation hazard. If a child under 3 will be using the blanket, you can embroider tentacles onto the background square instead.

KELP.

YARN.
Scheepjes Catona
412 (Forest Green)

NOTES.
- Strictly speaking, kelp is not a plant — it's a kind of algae. So although kelp's parts look planty, they function differently. Thus, leaves are actually "blades" and the main stalk is a "stipe".
- The kelp is worked in one continuous row. You start at the bottom, working blades up one side of the stipe then back down the other side.
- St counts for each blade do not include the stipe.

PATTERN.

SPECIAL STITCHES
To work a blade tip:
Sl st in second ch from hook, dc in next st, htr in next st, tr in next st, htr in next st, dc in next st. [6 sts]

BLADE TIP

KELP FROND
Using **412 (Forest Green)**:

Blade 1 Ch15, work blade tip, sl st in next 3 chs, 5 chs unworked. [9 sts]
Blade 2 Ch15, work blade tip, sl st in next 5 chs, 3 chs unworked. [11 sts]
Blade 3 Repeat Blade 2. [11 sts]
Blade 4 Ch9, work blade tip, sl st in next 2 chs. [8 sts]
Blade 5 Ch12, work blade tip, sl st in next 5 chs, skip last st of Blade 3, sl st in next 3 chs. [11 sts]

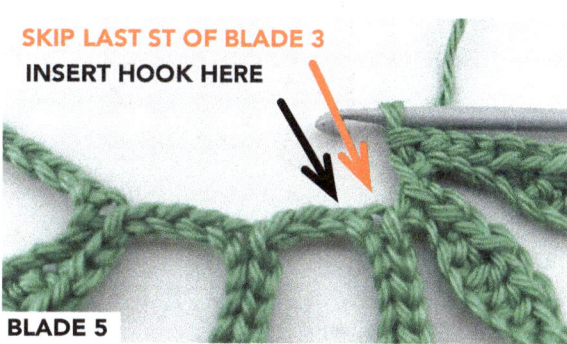

SKIP LAST ST OF BLADE 3
INSERT HOOK HERE

BLADE 5

Blade 6 Repeat Blade 5, skipping last st of Blade 2. [11 sts]
Blade 7 Ch10, work blade tip, sl st in next 3 sts, skip last st of Blade 1, sl st in last 5 sts. [9 sts]

Fasten off and weave in ends.

ARRANGING YOUR KELP
You may find your blade tips are curling and pointing in different directions. Give them a tug to ease them into shape. You will be able to stitch them down into place when you sew them onto their background square (see *Finishing Off* on page 68).

LOGGERHEAD SEA TURTLE.

YARN.
Scheepjes Catona
507 (Chocolate)   179 (Topaz)
Scheepjes Maxi Sweet Treat
404 (English Tea)   110 (Black)

NOTES.
- When you stitch your turtle onto its background square, angle the front flippers closer to the shell.
- Lightly stuff the shell with polyester stuffing.
- The front flippers use the same pattern. One flipper is stitched on upside-down to make a mirror image of the other.

PATTERN.

SHELL
Using **507 (Chocolate)**, ch6.

Row 1 (RS) 2dc in second ch from hook, dc in each of the next 3 chs, 2dc in last ch. Turn. [7 sts]
Row 2 (WS) Ch1 (does not count as a st throughout), 2dc, dc in each st until 1 st remains, 2dc in last st. Turn. [9 sts]
Row 3 Repeat Row 2. [11 sts]
Row 4 Repeat Row 2. [13 sts]
Row 5 Ch1, dc in each st to end. Turn. [13 sts]
Row 6 Ch1, dc in first st, BLO dc2tog, dc in each st to end. Turn. [12 sts]
Row 7 Ch1, dc in first st, FLO dc2tog, dc in each st to end. Turn. [11 sts]
Row 8 Repeat Row 6. [10 sts]
Row 9 Repeat Row 7. [9 sts]
Row 10 Repeat Row 6. [8 sts]
Row 11 Repeat Row 7. [7 sts]
Row 12 Ch1, dc in first st, BLO dc2tog, dc in next st, BLO dc2tog, dc in last st. Turn. [5 sts]
Row 13 Ch1, FLO dc2tog, dc in next st, FLO dc2tog. Turn. [3 sts]
Row 14 Ch1, dc in first st, skip next st, sl st into last st. [2 sts]

Fasten off.

HEAD
The head is worked up from the unworked side of the foundation ch of the shell.

Using **179 (Topaz)**, join yarn in second ch of foundation ch. Ch1.

Row 1 (RS) Dc in first st and next 2 chs. Turn. [3 sts]
Row 2 (WS) 2dc in first st, dc in next st, 2dc in last st. Turn. [5 sts]
Row 3 Do not work a turning ch, sl st in first st, dc in next st, htr in next st, dc in next st, sl st in last st. [5 sts]

Fasten off.

FRONT FLIPPERS — MAKE 2 THE SAME

The front flippers are worked separately then sewn onto the shell.

The left and right flippers are the same; reverse one when sewing it on.

Using **179 (Topaz)**, ch12.

Row 1 Sl st in second ch from hook and next st, dc in next 5 chs, skip 2 chs, dc in last 2 chs. Turn. [9 sts]
Row 2 Ch1, dc in first st, skip 2 sts, dc in next st, sl st in next 2 sts, 5 sts unworked. [4 sts]

Fasten off, leaving a 10cm tail. Use the tail to sew flipper onto shell at Rows 2-4. Repeat for other flipper, flipping it over when sewing it onto the shell.

BACK FLIPPERS

The back flippers are worked along the edges of the shell, into the ends of the shell rows. Treat each row end as a st.

Using **Topaz**, join yarn to the body as follows:

- Left flipper: in last st of Row 12
- Right flipper: in last st of Row 13

Row 1 (RS) Ch2, 2htr in st at base of ch, sl st into next st.

Fasten off. Repeat for other back flipper.

EYES

Using **Maxi Sweet Treat 110 Black** and a tapestry needle, stitch a French knot for each eye (see *Techniques* on page 13). Place them on Row 3, 2 sts apart, using the main photo as a guide. Weave in ends.

SHELL EMBROIDERY

The embroidery on the shell looks complicated but there is an straightforward method to it. Don't aim for perfection: wonky and uneven stitches will enhance the tortoiseshell effect. Use **Maxi Sweet Treat 404 (English Tea)** and a tapestry needle.

1

First, embroider a line around the edge of the shell. Make your stitches 1-2 crochet rows/stitches long (mix it up for variety). Then stitch a pointy rectangle down from the edges of the head, meeting two rows up from the pointy end of the shell.

2

Second, embroider 12-14 long stitches from the pointy rectangle out to the edge. You want them to fan out from the centre, roughly mirrored across both sides of the pointy rectangle.

3

Third, embroider 6-7 long stitches horizontally down the length of the pointy rectangle. Place some to meet the long stitches of the previous step, but not all. Fasten off and weave in all ends.

Sew your loggerhead sea turtle onto its background square (see *Finishing Off* on page 68).

LOGGERHEAD SEA TURTLE.

MANTA RAY.

YARN.
Scheepjes Catona
242 (Metal Grey)   106 (Snow White)
Scheepjes Maxi Sweet Treat
074 (Mercury)   110 (Black)

NOTES.
- The body is worked first; the tail and upturned white pectoral fin are then worked onto the edge of the body.
- The cephalic fins (the horn thingies on the head) are worked along on Row 8.
- When you stitch your manta ray onto its background square, lightly stuff the body with polyester stuffing.

PATTERN.

SPECIAL STITCHES
To work a cephalic fin:
(htr, ch4, sl st into fourth ch from hook, htr) in the same st.

BODY
Using **242 (Metal Grey)**, ch2.

Row 1 (WS) 2dc in second ch from hook. Turn. [2 sts]
Row 2 (RS) Ch1 (does not count as a st throughout), 2dc in each st to end. Turn. [4 sts]
Row 3 Repeat Row 2. [8 sts]
Row 4 Ch1, 2dc in first st, dc in each st until 1 st remains, 2dc in last st. Turn. [10 sts]
Row 5 Repeat Row 4. [12 sts]
Row 6 Dc in each st to end, ch5. Turn. [12 sts]
Row 7 Sl st in second ch from hook and next ch, dc in next 2 chs, 2dc in next st (on body), dc in each st until 1 st remains, 2dc in last st. Turn. [18 sts]
Row 8 Ch1, dc in first 6 sts, work cephalic fin, dc in next 2 sts, work cephalic fin, dc in next 3 sts, sl st in next 4 sts, 1 st unworked. [15 sts + 2 cephalic fins]

Fasten off.

UNDERSIDE OF PECTORAL FIN
Using **106 (Snow White)** and with WS facing, join yarn in fifth st from end of Row 8. Ch1.

Row 1 Skip st at base of ch, FLO dc in next 4 sts, ch4. Rotate work 180°. [4 sts, ch4]
Row 2 Dc in second ch from hook and next ch, skip next ch, sl st into end of Body Row 7. Fasten off.

WS

TAIL

Using **242 (Metal Grey),** join yarn to top of body at Row 4. Ch10, sl st in second ch from hook and each ch to end, sl st to next st on body.

Fasten off.

SPOTS

Using **Maxi Sweet Treat 074 (Mercury)** and a tapestry needle, stitch around 8 French knots onto the body, using the photo above as a guide. See *Techniques* on page 13)

EYES

Using **Maxi Sweet Treat 110 (Black)** and a tapestry needle, stitch a French knot for each eye. Place them on Row 3, 2 sts apart, using the main photo as a guide.

Weave in all ends and sew your manta ray onto its background square (see *Finishing Off* on page 68).

HOW BIG IS A MANTA RAY?
Manta rays can grow to a whopping 7m (23 ft) from wingtip to wingtip. They have the largest brain size of any fish and a very large brain-to-mass ratio. Don't worry, though - these gentle giants feed on plankton.

NARWHAL.

YARN.
Scheepjes Catona
242 (Metal Grey)   106 (Snow White)
172 (Pale Silver)
Scheepjes Maxi Sweet Treat
110 (Black)

NOTES.
- The head is worked in turned rows around both sides of the foundation ch.
- When you work the mid-row colour change, drop unused colour to pick up again later.
- Row 4 uses spike stitches, where you insert your hook into the corresponding next st on the previous row.

PATTERN.

HEAD
Using **106 (Snow White)**, ch7.

Row 1 (RS) Dc in second ch from hook and in next 4 sts, 3dc in last st; working back down the unworked side of the foundation ch, dc in last 5 sts. Turn. [13 sts]

Row 2 (WS) Ch1 (does not count as a st throughout), dc in first 6 sts, 3dc in next st, dc in last 6 sts. Turn. [15 sts]

Row 3 Ch1, dc in first 7 sts, 3dc in next st, dc in last 7 sts. Turn. [17 sts]

Row 4 Ch1, dc in first 8 sts, 3dc in next st, change to **242 (Metal Grey)**, dropping Snow White to pick up later; (dc in next st, dc in next st of previous row) 4 times to end. [19 sts]

Row 5 Ch1, dc in first 9 sts, 3dc in next st, change to **Snow White**, dc in last 9 sts. [21 sts]

Fasten off and weave in ends.

TUSK
Using **172 (Pale Silver)**, join yarn to middle st of 3-dc group of Row 5. Ch12.

Row 1 (RS) Sl st in second ch from hook and in each st to end, sl st into next st on body. [11 sts]

Cut yarn, leaving a 20cm tail for stitching the tusk onto the background square.

EYE

Using **Maxi Sweet Treat 110 (Black)** and a tapestry needle, work a French knot for an eye (see *Techniques* on page 13). Place it on Row 1 in the 3-dc group, using the main photo as a guide.

Keep your needle threaded to work the mouth.

MOUTH

The mouth continues on from the eye.

Work a long stitch from below the tusk to just past the eye. Curve it slightly, then secure the line with 3 little tacking stitches down its length. Use the main photo as a guide. Fasten off and weave in all ends.

ARRANGING YOUR NARWHAL

Sew your narwhal onto its background square (see *Finishing Off* on page 68). Stuff the head lightly with polyester stuffing. Secure the tusk with a series of short diagonal stitches using the tusk yarn tail. Use the main photo as a guide.

> **THE UNICORN OF THE SEA.**
> The narwhal's impressive tusk is actually an overgrown canine tooth. Mostly (though not exclusively) found on males, tusks can grow to a length of 2-3m (4.9-10ft). In rare cases, a narwhal grows two tusks. Much is unknown about the function of a narwhal's tusk. They may be used as a way of communicating or as a sensor to detect temperature, water pressure and salinity. The tusk is flexible and able to bend about 30cm (1 ft) without breaking.

OCTOPUS.

YARN.
Scheepjes Catona
  252 (Watermelon)
Scheepjes Maxi Sweet Treat
  238 (Powder Pink)
  110 (Black)

NOTES.
- The head is worked in turned rows around both sides of the foundation ch.
- The arms are continued on from the head and are worked along its edge in two rows.
- The suckers are embroidered on by running a line of yarn under the stitches of the arms.

PATTERN

HEAD
Using **252 (Watermelon)**, ch7.

Row 1 (RS) Dc in second ch from hook and in next 4 sts, 3dc in last st; working back down the unworked side of the foundation ch, dc in last 5 sts. Turn. [13 sts]
Row 2 (WS) Ch1 (does not count as a st throughout), dc in first 6 sts, 3dc in next st, dc in last 6 sts. Turn. [15 sts]
Row 3 Ch1, dc in first 5 sts, htr in next st, 2tr in next 3 sts, htr, dc in next 4 sts, ch3, sl st into third ch from hook (eye bump made), dc in last st. [18 sts]

Leave loop on hook for arms.

ARMS
The arms are crocheted into the row ends of the head; four arms are worked on the RS along the front and then, turning, four arms on the WS underneath.

Space your arms evenly across the straight edge, skipping a head row if necessary.

FRONT ARMS
Ch 16, sl st in second ch from hook, dc in each st to end. Sl st in next 2 sts on head.

Repeat three more times, working the last sl st into the first st of Row 3. After Arm 4, turn.

ARM 1

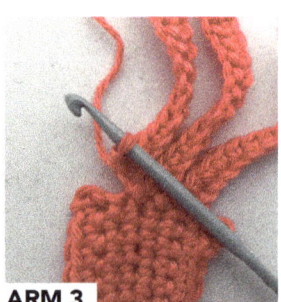
ARM 3

ARM 4

EYE
Using **Maxi Sweet Treat 110 (Black)** and a tapestry needle, stitch a French knot into centre of eye surround (see *Techniques* on page 13). Fasten off.

SUCKERS
The suckers are worked by running a length of yarn under the stitches on the WS of each arm.

Using **Maxi Sweet Treat 238 (Powder Pink)** and a tapestry needle, start yarn on WS at base of any arm. Insert needle under the straight legs only of each st along arm (see diagram below).

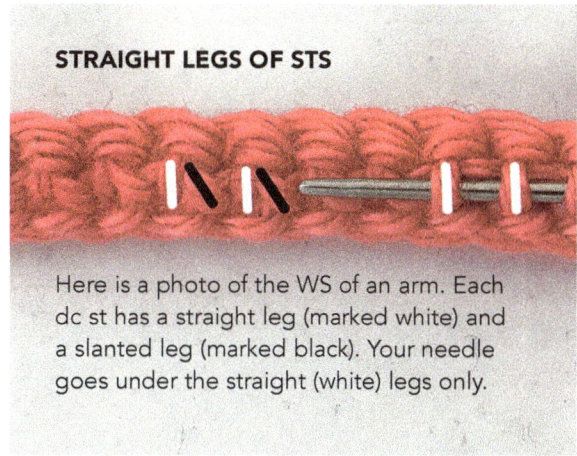
STRAIGHT LEGS OF STS

Here is a photo of the WS of an arm. Each dc st has a straight leg (marked white) and a slanted leg (marked black). Your needle goes under the straight (white) legs only.

BACK ARMS
The back arms are worked into the WS of the front arm sts (see diagram below). Even spacing of the arms is not so critical on the back – insert your hook under one of the loops however you can. Aim to end up in the st just before the eye bump.

To set up Ch1, insert hook into loop under the first arm, sl st.

Work 4 back arms as for front. Fasten off.

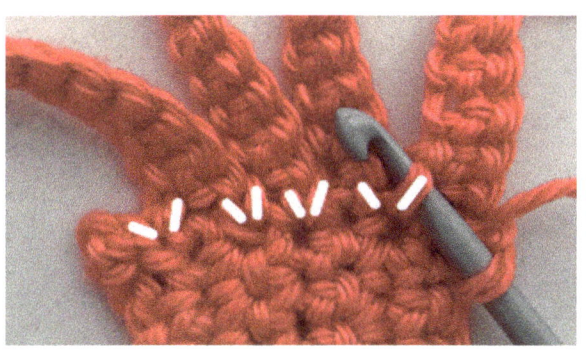

At the end of each arm, secure your yarn under the last st and return back along the arm, inserting your needle under the same sts. Weave in all ends.

EYE SURROUND
Using **Watermelon**, make a magic loop.

Rnd 1 Ch1, 6dc into the loop. [6 sts]

Fasten off and use yarn tails to sew eye surround onto the head at Row 2 at the lower edge near the arms. The eye bump you made at Row 3 suggests the other eye.

ARRANGING YOUR OCTOPUS
The front arms may splay away from the back arms. When sewing your octopus onto its background square (see *Finishing Off* on page 68), stitch down the arms where they join the body. Leave the ends of the arms loose to curl up randomly. Make sure the eye bump sticks out a little bit from the head.

OCTOPUS.

PORCUPINE PUFFER.

YARN.
Scheepjes Catona
245 (Green Yellow)   106 (Snow White)
Scheepjes Maxi Sweet Treat
110 (Black)

NOTES.
- This creature is worked in rnds joined with a sl st. From Rnd 2 onwards, work a mid-row colour change and carry your unused colour along under your stitches.
- The fins are worked separately into the last rnd.
- The spines are embroidered on once you've sewn your porcupine puffer onto its background square.

PATTERN

HEAD / BODY
When changing colour, carry unused yarn along under your sts to be picked up as needed. From Rnd 2 onwards, use the new colour to work the last yarn over on the last st of the rnd so the joining sl st is worked in the new colour.

Using **245 (Green Yellow),** make a magic loop.

Rnd 1 Ch1 (does not count as a st throughout), 6dc into the loop. Sl st to first st to join. [6 sts]
Rnd 2 Ch1, 2dc in each of first 3 sts; change to **106 (Snow White),** 2dc in each of last 3 sts. Sl st to join. [12 sts]
Rnd 3 Change to **Green Yellow**. Ch1, (dc, 2dc in the next st) 6 times, changing to **Snow White** after 9 sts. Sl st to join. [18 sts]
Rnd 4 Change to **Green Yellow**. Ch1, (dc in next 2 sts, 2dc in next st) 6 times, changing to **Snow White** after 12 sts. Sl st to join. [24 sts]
Rnd 5 Change to **Green Yellow**. Ch1, (dc in next 3 sts, 2dc in the next st) 6 times, changing to **Snow White** after 15 sts. Sl st to join. [30 sts]

Change to **Green Yellow** and keep loop on hook.

FINS
The first fin is continued on from Rnd 5.

Row 1 (RS) Ch3, 5tr in st at base of ch, ch3, sl st to same st. Fasten off.

For second fin, rejoin yarn on other side in last Green Yellow st. Repeat Row 1.

EYES

Using **Maxi Sweet Treat 110 (Black)** and a tapestry needle, work 2 French knots for eyes (see *Techniques* on page 13). Place them between Rows 3 and 4 at the edge of the Green Yellow section, using the main photo as a guide.

Weave in all ends.

SPINES

The spines are embroidered on after you've sewn your porcupine puffer onto its background square (see *Finishing Off* on page 68). Stitch a series of short lines around the edge of the circle, one spine for each stitch. Vary the lengths a little. Use **Catona Green Yellow** and **Snow White**, matching the colour of the spines to the crochet sts and referring to the main photo as a guide.

WHAT IS A PORCUPINE PUFFER?

In a word, awesome. To avoid predators, the porcupine puffer can swallow large quantities of water (or sometimes air) and inflate into a spherical ball up to three times its usual size. Long spines radiate outwards from its skin, which turn it into an unpalatable dinner for most predators. Some species of porcupine puffer are also poisonous; their internal organs contain a neurotoxin up to 1,200 times more potent than cyanide. Despite this, porcupine puffers are regarded as a delicacy in many parts of the world. In Japan, for example, chefs licensed to prepare *fugu* must train rigorously for three years before they can serve the dish.

QUAHOG.

YARN.
Scheepjes Catona
 254 (Moon Rock) 395 (Willow)
 179 (Topaz)
Scheepjes Maxi Sweet Treat
 404 (English Tea)

NOTES.
- A quahog is a type of edible clam found on the east cost of North and Central America. Pronounced *kwah-hog* or *ko-hog*, I think, but it's hotly contested.
- No need to cut your yarn between stripes; just drop it and pick it up as required.
- The fine lines are embroidered on afterwards.

PATTERN

SHELL
When changing colour, drop unused colour to pick up later as required.

Using **254 (Moon Rock)**, ch2.
Row 1 (RS) 2dc in second ch from hook. Turn. [2 sts]
Row 2 (WS) Ch1 (does not count as a st throughout), 2dc in each st to end. Turn. [4 sts]

Change to **395 (Willow)**.
Row 3 Ch1, 2dc in first st, dc in each st until 1 st remains, 2dc in last st. Turn. [6 sts]

Change to **179 (Topaz)**.
Row 4 Repeat Row 3. [8 sts]

Change to **Moon Rock**.
Row 5 Repeat Row 3. [10 sts]
Row 6 Ch1, dc in each st to end. Turn. [10 sts]

Change to **Topaz**.
Row 7 Ch1, 2dc in first st, dc in next 2 sts, htr in next st, tr in next 2 sts, htr in next st, dc in next 2 sts, 2dc in last st. [12 sts]

Change to **Willow**.
Row 8 Repeat Row 6. [12 sts]

Change to **Moon Rock**.
Row 9 Ch1, 2dc in first st, dc in each st to end. Turn. [13 sts]
Row 10 Ch1, dc in first 4 sts, htr in next st, tr in next 2 sts, htr in next st, dc in next 4 sts, 2dc in last st. Turn. [14 sts]

Change to **Willow**.
Row 11 Ch1, dc in first 3 sts, htr in next st, tr in next 6 sts, htr in next st, dc in last 3 sts. [14 sts]

Fasten off and weave in ends.

Unsightly yarn floats along the edge? You'll be able to hide them with your stitches when you sew your quahog on its background square (see *Finishing Off* on page 68).

FINE LINES
Using **Maxi Sweet Treat 404 (English Tea)** and a tapestry needle, embroider a line of stitches along Rows 7 and 10. Fasten off and weave in all ends.

RED CRAB.

YARN.
Scheepjes Catona
　516 (Candy Apple)
Scheepjes Maxi Sweet Treat
　110 (Black)

NOTES.
- The claws are worked separately then stitched onto the carapace.
- The legs are embroidered on once you've sewn your crab onto its background square.

PATTERN.

CARAPACE
Using **516 (Candy Apple)**, ch5.

Row 1 Dc in second ch from hook and in each ch to end. Turn. [4 sts]
Row 2 Ch1 (does not count as a st throughout), 2dc in first st, dc in each st until 1 st remains, 2dc in last st. Turn. [6 sts]
Row 3 Repeat Row 2. [8 sts]
Row 4 Repeat Row 2. [10 sts]
Rows 5-7 Ch1, dc in each st to end. Turn. [10 sts]
Row 8 Ch1, BLO dc2tog, dc in next 6 sts, BLO dc2tog. Turn. [8 sts]
Row 9 Ch1, dc in first 2 sts, htr in next st, tr in next 3 sts, htr in next st, dc in last 2 sts. [8 sts]

Fasten off.

CLAWS
The claws are worked separately and stitched onto the completed carapace. Using **Candy Apple**:

LEFT CLAW Ch13, sl st in second ch from hook and next 2chs, ch6, sl st in second ch from hook and next 4 chs, dc in ch at base of ch, sl st in next 3 chs, dc in last 5 chs. Fasten off, leaving a 10cm tail for sewing.

RIGHT CLAW Ch15, sl st in second ch from hook and next 4 chs, ch4, sl st in second ch from hook and next 2chs, dc in ch at base of ch, sl st in next 3 chs, dc in last 5 chs. Fasten off, leaving a 10cm tail for sewing.

Sew claws onto either side of carapace at Rows 7 and 8, using the main photo as a guide.

ARRANGING YOUR RED CRAB
Sew your red crab onto its background square (see *Finishing Off* on page 68). Curl in the pincers in toward each other for a nice nippy claw.

The eyes and the zigzag line are embroidered with **Maxi Sweet Treat 110 (Black)** and a tapestry needle. You can work them without breaking your yarn (first eye, zigzag, second eye), but for convenience they are separated out below.

EYES
Work 2 French knots for eyes (see *Techniques* on page 13). Place them at the edge of Row 9 in the first and last sts, using the main photo as a guide.

ZIGZAG LINE
Embroider a zigzag line of stitches on the carapace along Row 8, using the main photo as a guide. Fasten off.

Weave in all ends.

CRAB CROSSINGS
Red crabs live on Christmas Island, Australia and nowhere else — up to 50 million of them. When the rainy season starts around October, they all begin a legendary mass migration from their forest habitat to breeding grounds on the shore. They pour out over any obstacle in their way, including busy roads. During this time, the human inhabitants of Christmas Island set up road closures, fences and crab tunnels to minimise crustaceous casualties.

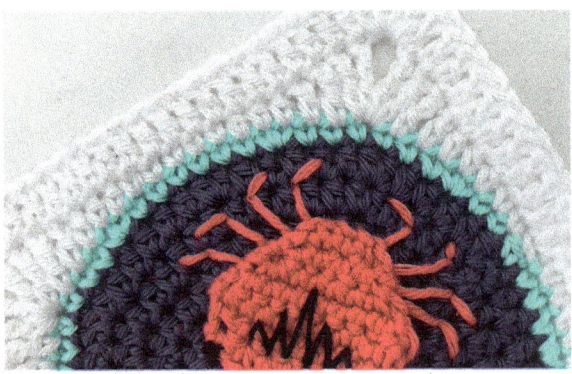

LEGS
The legs are embroidered onto the background square in **Candy Apple** using a tapestry needle. Work 4 legs between Rows 1 and 3, making 2 sts per leg. Repeat for the other side. Use the photo above and the main photo as a guide.

SEA SLUG.

YARN.

Scheepjes Catona
- 511 (Cornflower)
- 208 (Yellow Gold)
- 281 (Tangerine)
- 106 (Snow White)
- 110 (Black)

NOTES.
- The foot is worked in a continuous spiral around both sides of the foundation ch, leaving a line of unworked loops. Do not join rnds with a sl st or work a turning ch.
- The frill is worked up from the unworked loops and finished with a line of embroidered stitches.
- The horns are worked separately and then stitched on.

PATTERN.

FOOT
(THE BODY BIT)
Using **511 (Cornflower)**, ch11.

Rnd 1 Dc in second ch from hook and in next 8 chs, 3dc in last ch; working back down the unworked side of the foundation ch, dc in next 8chs, 2dc in last ch. [22 sts]

Rnd 2 Dc in first 10 sts; working in BLO for rest of rnd, 3dc in next st, dc in next 10 sts, 3dc in last st. [26 sts]

Rnd 3 Dc in first st, htr in next st, 3tr in next st, htr in next st, dc in next 3 sts, htr in next 2 sts, dc in next st, sl st in next st, 15 sts unworked. [13 sts]

Fasten off.

FRILL
The frill is worked into the unworked loops on Row 2. Using **106 (Snow White)** and with RS facing, join yarn to first unworked loop.

Row 1 (RS) Ch1 (does not count as a st throughout), 2dc in each st to end. [24 sts]

Change to **208 (Yellow Gold)**. Cut Snow White, leaving a 30cm tail.

Row 2 (WS) Ch1, dc in first st, (2dc in next st, dc in next st) 7 times to end. [36 sts]

Fasten off.

Using the **Snow White** yarn tail and a tapestry needle, embroider a line of stitches along Row 2, just under the back loop. Fasten off.

Using **110 (Black)** and a tapestry needle, embroider a line of stitches along Row 1, where the blue stitches meet the white stitches. Fasten off.

RHINOPHORES — MAKE 2 THE SAME (THE TWO HORNS AT THE FRONT)
Using **281 (Tangerine)** and a crochet hook, ch5.

Row 1 Sl st in second ch from hook and next 2 chs, dc in last ch. Fasten off.

Stitch rhinophores to Rnd 3, positioning one behind the foot. Use the photo below and the main photo as a guide.

GILLS (THE TENTACLES AT THE BACK)
Cut three length of **Tangerine**, about 6cm long. Fold double and knot each one on to the foot at Rnd 3, in the middle tr of the 3tr-group.

Sew your sea slug onto its background square (see *Finishing Off* on page 68).

WHOA. THAT'S A SEA SLUG?
Actually a kind of nudibranch, which is a type of sea slug. Not your bog-standard garden variety slug, are they? Nudibranches are the fabulous little peacocks of the sea. There are over 3000 recognised species and they come in a mindblowing range of colours and forms.

Go and Google them right now. You can thank me later.

WARNING
The knots attaching the gills can loosen over time, freeing the strands of yarn. This is a potential choking or inhalation hazard. If a child under 3 will be using the blanket, you can embroider gills onto the background square instead.

TUBE WORMS.

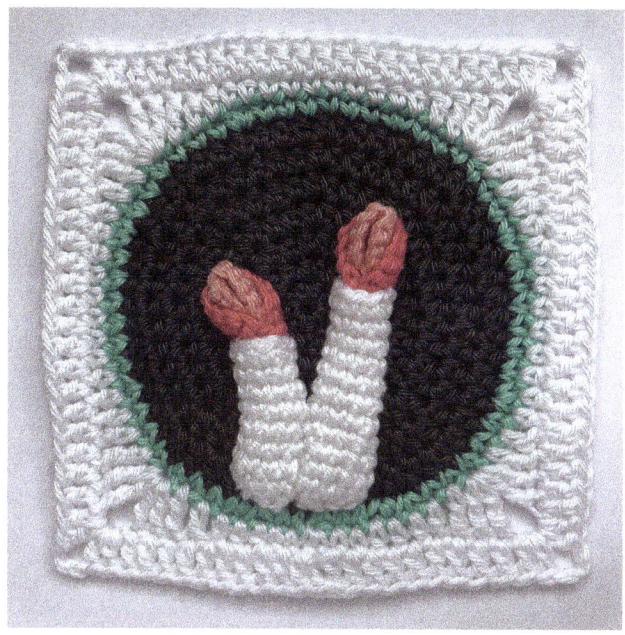

YARN.
Scheepjes Catona
- 106 (Snow White)
- 518 (Marshmallow)
- 114 (Shocking Pink)

NOTES.
- The tubes of this creature is not crocheted flat. They are worked in the round in a continuous spiral, with no sl st to join each rnd.
- The pink plumes are worked separately (flat, in a continuous spiral) then stitched into the tubes.

PATTERN.

TUBES
The tubes are worked in continuous spiral. Use a loose tension for the starting ch so your tubes don't pinch in at the base.

Using **106 (Snow White),** ch8.

TUBE 1
Rnd 1 Dc in first ch to form a loop, and in each ch to end. [8 sts]
Rnds 2-12 Dc in each st to end.

Fasten off, leaving a 20cm tail for sewing.

TUBE 2
Repeat Tube 1, working 8 rnds only.

PLUMES — MAKE 2 THE SAME (THE PINK BITS)
Each plume is made up of two pieces, an inner part and an outer part. The two parts are folded together and stitched into the tubes.

INNER PART
Using **518 (Marshmallow),** make a magic loop.

Rnd 1 Ch1 (does not count as a st), 6dc into the loop. [6 sts]
Rnd 2 2dc in each st around. [12 sts]

Fasten off.

OUTER PART
Using **114 (Shocking Pink),** make a magic loop.

Rnd 1 Ch1 (does not count as a st), 6dc into the loop. [6 sts]
Rnd 2 2dc in each st around. [12 sts]
Rnd 3 (Dc, 2dc in next st) 6 times to end. [18 sts]

Fasten off, leaving a 20cm tail for sewing.

To make up the plume, lay the inner part on top of the outer part, both RS uppermost. Pinch them together so that the two parts fold up, tweaking the inner part up so it protrudes out the top slightly. Use the outer part yarn tail to work a few stitches at one edge to secure the parts together.

Insert the pinched section into the top of tube (a jab with pointy scissors can help), and use the tube yarn tail to stitch it in securely.

ARRANGING YOUR TUBE WORMS
Sew your tube worms onto their background square (see *Finishing Off* on page 68). Splay them out away from each other at the top.

UMM... WHY THOUGH?
Tube worms, bless their little cotton socks, aren't the cuddliest of creatures, are they? But they are pretty cool. They grow up to 2.4m (7ft 10in) long and live in the toxic chemical soup emitted by hydrothermal vents. They tolerate extremely high levels of hydrogen sulfide (that very poisonous, very corrosive chemical compound that smells like rotten eggs). Their plume is a specialised organ for filtering nutrients.

URCHIN.

YARN.

Scheepjes Catona
 242 (Metal Grey)
 172 (Pale Silver)
 253 (Tropic)
Scheepjes Maxi Sweet Treat
 404 (English Tea)

NOTES.
- Most of the work for this creature is done once you've sewn it onto its background square. Stuff it lightly with polyester stuffing as you do so.
- Radiate the spines out from the centre of the urchin. Make your stitches a bit haphazard for a more natural look.

PATTERN.

TEST
(THE HARD SHELL BIT)
Using **242 (Metal Grey)**, ch5.

Row 1 Dc in second ch from hook and in each ch to end. Turn. [4 sts]
Row 2 Ch1 (does not count as a st throughout), dc in each st until 1 st remains, 2dc in last st. Turn. [5 sts]
Row 3 Ch1, 2dc in first st, dc in each to end. Turn. [6 sts]
Row 4 Repeat Row 2. [7 sts]
Rows 5-10 Ch1, dc in each st to end. Turn. [7 sts]
Row 11 Ch1, FLO dc2tog, dc in each st to end. Turn. [6 sts]
Row 12 Ch1, dc in each st until 2 sts remain, BLO dc2tog. Turn. [5 sts]
Row 13 Repeat Row 11. [4 sts]

Fasten off and weave in ends.

SPINES
The spines are embroidered on once you've sewn your urchin onto its background square (see *Finishing Off* on page 68).

First, use **172 (Pale Silver)** to embroider stitches radiating out from the centre of the urchin. Make the stitches 1-2 crochet sts long.

1

2

Second, use **253 (Tropic)** to add further sts, longer than the first sts and mainly within the edges of the test.

3

Third, use **Maxi Sweet Treat 404 (English Tea)** to add a series of long sts mainly around the edge of the test, with 3-4 sts in the middle. Weave in all ends.

LOOKING SHARP.

There are around 200 species of sea urchin and they can be found in oceans around the world. They typically range in size from 3-10cm (1-4in). They are omnivorous and have a specialised mouth, located on their underside, that can drill into rock. They can regenerate their spines if they need to.

VAMPIRE SQUID.

YARN.
Scheepjes Catona
516 (Candy Apple)
252 (Watermelon)
511 (Cornflower)

NOTES.
- The body is worked first in turned rows, then the arms.
- The cloak (the bit in between the arms) is worked in sections along each arm, and then sewn to the adjacent arm.

PATTERN.

BODY
Using **518 (Candy Apple),** ch4.

Row 1 (RS) Dc in second ch from hook and in each ch to end. Turn. [3 sts]
Row 2 (WS) Ch1 (does not count as a st throughout), 2dc in each st to end. Turn. [6 sts]
Row 3 Ch1, dc in each st to end. Turn. [6 sts]
Row 4 Ch1, 2dc in first st, dc in each st to end. Turn. [7 sts]
Rows 5-7 Repeat Row 3. [7 sts]
Row 8 Ch1, BLO dc2tog, dc in next 3 sts, BLO dc2tog. Turn. [5 sts]
Row 9 Repeat Row 3. [5 sts]

The arms are worked on from Row 9.

ARMS
With WS facing:

Arm 1 Ch10, sl st in second ch from hook and in each ch to end, dc in next st on body.
Arm 2 Ch11, sl st in second ch from hook and in each ch to end, dc in next st on body.
Arm 3 Repeat Arm 2.
Arm 4 Repeat Arm 1, working a sl st to the end of Row 9 to join to the body.

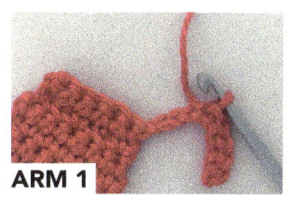
ARM 1

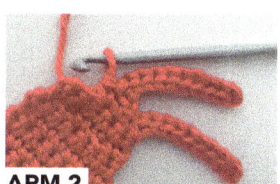
ARM 2

ARM 4

55   VAMPIRE SQUID.

FIN

The fin is worked separately and sewn onto the body. Using **Candy Apple**, ch4.

Row 1 Htr in third ch from hook, dc in last st. Fasten off.

Sew fin to the body in the second st of Row 4, using the photo below and the main photo as a guide.

CLOAK

The cloak is worked in sections along each arm, and then stitched together into one piece. Each row is worked into the back loops of the sl sts (see photo below). The sl sts can be tight to work into. You can make life easier before you begin by using a tapestry needle to "lift" the sts you'll be working into.

Using **252 (Watermelon)** and with RS facing, join yarn to Arm 1 at the sl st nearest the body and ch1.

Row 1 Dc in first st, htr in next st, tr in next 5 sts, 2 sts unworked. Fasten off leaving a 10cm tail for sewing.

Repeat for Arms 2 and 3, leaving 3 sts unworked at the end of the row. Leave Arm 4 unworked.

Once all cloak sections have been completed and with WS facing, use the yarn tails to sew each section of the cloak to the adjacent arm.

WS   **RS**

EYE

Using **511 (Cornflower)** and a tapestry needle, stitch a French knot for the eye (see *Techniques* on page 13). Place it on Row 8 at the second st, using the main photo as a guide.

Weave in all ends. Sew your vampire squid onto its background square (see *Finishing Off* on page 68).

COUNT SQUIDULA?

The vampire squid lurks in the extreme deep, but isn't quite as scary as it sounds. Growing to only around 30cm (1 ft) long, it has rows of fleshy, harmless spines on the inside of its cloak. If threatened, the vampire squid inverts itself into its cloak. Despite its name, it doesn't suck blood, feeding instead on organic debris. It detects and captures its food with two long filaments that it extends from its body, rather like a fishing line.

WALRUS.

YARN.
Scheepjes Catona
 254 (Moon Rock)   106 (Snow White)
Scheepjes Maxi Sweet Treat
 404 (English Tea)   110 (Black)

NOTES.
- The head is worked first in a continuous spiral, with no sl st to join each rnd. The body continues on from the head and is worked in turned rows.
- The snout, tusks and flippers are all worked separately and then stitched onto the head and body.
- The whiskers are embroidered on.

PATTERN.

HEAD
The head is worked in a continuous spiral, with no sl st to join each rnd.

Using **254 (Moon Rock)**, make a magic loop.

Rnd 1 Ch1 (does not count as a st), 6dc into the loop. [6 sts]
Rnd 2 2dc in each st to end. [12 sts]
Rnd 3 (Dc, 2dc in next st) 6 times. [18 sts]
Rnd 4 (Dc in next 2 sts, 2dc in next st) 6 times. [24 sts]

BODY
The body continues on from the head and is worked in turned rows.

Row 1 Ch3, 2tr in first st, 2htr in next st, dc in next 3 sts, 2htr in next st, 2tr in next st, dtr in next st, 16 sts unworked. Turn. [12 sts]
Row 2 Ch1, 3dc in first st, dc in next 10 sts, dc in top of ch3. Turn. [14 sts]
Rows 3-6 Ch1, dc in each st to end. [14 sts]
Row 7 Ch1, dc in first 3 sts, htr in each st until 3 sts remain, dc in last 3 sts. [14 sts]

Fasten off.

ROW 1

TUSKS — MAKE 2 THE SAME
Using **106 (Snow White)**, ch8. Fasten off, leaving a 10cm tail for sewing.

Sew the tusks onto the middle of the head at Rnd 2, one st apart. Use the photo below as a guide.

SNOUT

The snout is worked in a continuous spiral, with no sl st to join each rnd. Using **Moon Rock**, make a magic loop.

Rnd 1 Ch1 (does not count as a st), 8dc into the loop. [8 sts]
Rnd 2 Dc in each st around. Fasten off, leaving a 15cm tail for sewing.

Squash the snout into an oval and sew it onto the head over the top of the tusks.

VIBRASSAE (THE WHISKERS)

The vibrassae are embroidered on using **Maxi Sweet Treat 404 (English Tea)** and a tapestry needle.

Work a series of stitches over the snout radiating out and down from the centre. Make some of the stitches cross from the snout onto the head. Use the photo below and the main photo as a guide.

EYES AND NOSTRILS

Stitch 2 French knots for eyes (see *Techniques* on page 13). Place them at the edge of the snout, using the main photo as a guide.

Add two small stitches for nostrils on top of the snout, again using the main photo as a guide. Weave in ends.

LEFT

RIGHT

FLIPPERS

The flippers are worked separately and sewn onto the body. Using **Moon Rock**, ch2.

LEFT FLIPPER
Row 1 (RS) 3dc in second ch from hook. Turn. [3 sts]
Row 2 (WS) Ch1, dc in each st to end. Turn. [3 sts]
Row 3 Repeat Row 2.

Fasten off, leaving a 10cm tail for sewing.

RIGHT FLIPPER
Repeat left flipper, repeating Row 3 once more.

Sew flippers onto the body at Row 4, using the photo above and the main photo as a guide. Secure each flipper with a few stitches at the top and in the middle, so the bottom edges are free to curl a little.

Weave in all ends. Sew your walrus onto its background square (see *Finishing Off* on page 68).

WHAT ARE THOSE COOL TUSKS FOR?
Both male and female walruses have tusks, though the male's are usually bigger. Walruses use their tusks for displaying dominance, foraging for food and as tools. They hook their tusks over ice floes to haul themselves out of the water and break breathing holes when they're under the ice. Tusks typically grow to about 36cm (14in) long, though they can reach as long as 100cm (39in) in males.

AXOLOTL.

YARN.
Scheepjes Catona
    408 (Old Rose)   114 (Shocking Pink)
Scheepjes Maxi Sweet Treat
    110 (Black)

NOTES.
- The head is worked in the round in a continuous spiral around both sides of the foundation ch.
- The legs are worked directly on from the head.
- The gills and toes are embroidered on once you've sewn your axolotl onto its background square. Lightly stuff the head with polyester stuffing.

PATTERN

HEAD
The head is worked in a continuous spiral (no sl st to join) around both sides of the foundation ch.

Using **408 (Old Rose)**, ch4.

Rnd 1 Dc in second ch from hook and next ch, 3dc in last ch; working back down the unworked side of the foundation ch, dc in next ch, 2dc in last ch. [8 sts]
Rnd 2 2dc in first st, dc in next st, 2dc in next 3 sts, dc in next st, 2dc in next 2 sts. [14 sts]
Rnd 3 2dc in first st, dc in next 4 sts, 2dc in next 3 sts, dc in next 4 sts, 2dc in next 2 sts. [20 sts]
Rnd 4 2dc in first st, dc in next 7 sts, 2dc in next 3 sts, dc in next 7 sts, 2dc in next 2 sts. [26 sts]
Rnd 5 2dc in first st, dc in next 10 sts, 2dc in next 3 sts, dc in next 10 sts, 2dc in next 2 sts. [32 sts]

Leave loop on hook for legs.

LEGS
The legs continue on from Rnd 5. Dc in next 2 sts to get into position.

LEFT LEG
Ch9, sl st in second ch from hook, dc in next 3 chs, skip ch, dc in next 3 chs, sl st to next st on head.

Sl st in next 6 sts. If you think the position of the legs is looking unbalanced, you can add in 1-2 sl sts here.

RIGHT LEG
Ch8, sl st in second ch from hook, dc in next 2 chs, (dc, ch1, dc) in next ch, dc in next 3 chs, sl st to next st on head.

Fasten off. You will be able to tweak the angles of the legs and sew them down into the right place later. You may need to skew the head slightly when you do so. Keep this in mind when you stitch the face.

EYES AND MOUTH

Using **Maxi Sweet Treat 110 (Black)** and a tapestry needle, stitch 2 French knots for eyes (see *Techniques* on page 13). Place them on Rnd 3, roughly in line with the foundation ch.

Add a curving smile for the mouth between Rnds 2 and 3, 6 sts long. Work one long stitch, then secure it with 3 little tacking stitches along the length of the stitch. Use the photo below as a guide. Weave in all ends.

FEET

The feet are embroidered on as you stitch your axolotl onto its background square (see *Finishing Off* on page 68). Using **Old Rose** and a tapestry needle, stitch four toes onto the end of each leg. Use the photo below and the main photo as a guide.

GILLS (THE FEATHERY BITS)

The gills are embroidered on using **114 (Shocking Pink)** and a tapestry needle.

Work three gills on each side of the head. Each gill is made up of a main stem with 10-14 small stitches angled off it.

Use the photo below and the main photo as a guide.

DOESN'T AXOLOTL START WITH A?
Absolutely, dear reader! A bit of cheating here: axolotls don't start with X and they don't live under the sea (they're freshwater amphibians). But close enough. Those fabulous feathery gills are hard to resist, are they not? Axolotls are popular pets; if you have two or more, they like to pile up in the corner of their aquarium in "axie stacks".

YELLOW TANG.

YARN.
Scheepjes Catona
  280 (Lemon)
  245 (Green Yellow)
Scheepjes Maxi Sweet Treat
  110 (Black)

NOTES.
- The body is worked in rows.
- The BLO sts on Row 7 of the body leave unworked loops so you can work the pectoral fin up from them later.
- The fins are worked along the edge of the body rows.
- Contrast stitching is embroidered onto the tail and fins.

PATTERN.

BODY
Using **280 (Lemon)**, ch4.

Row 1 (RS) Tr in fourth ch from the hook. Turn. [1 st]
Row 2 (WS) Ch1 (does not count as a st throughout), dc in first st and in top of ch4. Turn. [2 sts]
Row 3 Ch1, 2dc in each st to end. Turn. [4 sts]
Row 4 Ch1, 2dc in first st, dc in next 2 sts, 2dc in last st. Turn. [6 sts]
Row 5 Ch1, 2dc in first st, dc in next 3 sts, 2dc in last 2 sts. Turn. [9 sts]
Row 6 Ch1, 2dc in first st, dc in each st to end. Turn. [10 sts]
Row 7 Ch1, dc in first 2 sts, BLO dc in next 2 sts, dc in each st to end. Turn. [10 sts]
Row 8 Ch1, BLO dc2tog, dc in each st to end. Turn. [9 sts]
Row 9 Ch1, dc in first 7 sts, FLO dc2tog. Turn. [8 sts]
Row 10 Ch1, dc in first 4 sts, BLO dc2tog, dc in last 2 sts. Turn. [7 sts]
Row 11 Ch1, dc in each st to end. Turn. [7 sts]
Row 12 Ch1, BLO dc2tog, dc in each st to end. Turn. [6 sts]
Row 13 Ch1, FLO dc2tog, dc in next 2 sts, FLO dc2tog. Turn. [4 sts]
Row 14 Ch1, BLO dc2tog, BLO dc2tog. Turn. [2 sts]

TAIL
The tail continues on from Row 14 of the body.

Row 1 (RS) Ch3, 2tr in each st to end. [4 sts]

Fasten off.

FINS

The fins are worked along the edges of the body into the ends of rows. Treat each row end as one st.

DORSAL FIN
(THE TOP ONE)

Using **Lemon**, join yarn to body in end of Row 13. Ch3.

Row 1 (RS) Dtr in next 2 sts, tr in next st, htr in next st, dc in next st, sl st in next st.

Fasten off.

ANAL FIN
(THE BOTTOM ONE)

Using **Lemon**, join yarn to body in end of Row 15. Ch2.

Row 1 (RS) Htr in first st, tr in each of next 4 sts, ch2, sl st to next st. Fasten off.

PECTORAL FIN
(THE ONE ON THE SIDE)

Using **Lemon**, join yarn to lowermost unworked loop on Row 7. Ch3.

Row 1 (RS) Tr in st at base of ch and in each st to end, ch 3, sl st into same st as last tr. Fasten off.

TAIL/FIN STITCHES

Using **245 (Green Yellow)** and a tapestry needle, work radiating stitches on the tail, dorsal, anal and pectoral fins.

Use the photo above and the main photo as a guide.

EYE

Using **Maxi Sweet Treat 110 (Black)** and a tapestry needle, work a French knot for an eye (see *Techniques* on page 13). Place it on Row 4 on the third st from the top, using the main photo as a guide.

Weave in all ends. Sew your yellow tang onto its background square (see *Finishing Off* on page 68).

> **SOMETHING COOL ABOUT YELLOW TANGS**
> And here it is: yellow tangs can change their colouration to deter predators. At night, their yellow colour will fade and a brownish patch and a white line will appear down their sides. They will brighten up again rapidly in daylight.

ZOOPLANKTON.

YARN. ☆☆☆

Scheepjes Catona
- 408 (Old Rose)
- 245 (Green Yellow)
- 397 (Cyan)
- 511 (Cornflower)
- 281 (Tangerine)
- 254 (Moon Rock)
- 114 (Shocking Pink)
- 412 (Forest Green)
- 179 (Topaz)

Scheepjes Maxi Sweet Treat
- 074 (Mercury)
- 404 (English Tea)

NOTES.
- This square is worked in both crochet and embroidery.
- For the crochet elements, work tight. Switch to a 2.5mm hook to stay small.
- Feel free to make up your own wriggly little thingies.

PATTERN.

GRANNY SQUARE

Using **408 (Old Rose)**, ch3 (counts as a htr). Work all sts into same ch.

Rnd 1 (RS) Htr in second ch from hook, ch2, (2htr, ch2) 3 times. Sl st into top of the ch3 to join. Fasten off, leaving a 30cm tail for sewing. Sew granny square onto background square and weave in ends.

CIRCLES WITH LEGS — MAKE 2 THE SAME

Using **397 (Cyan)** make a magic loop.

Rnd 1 (RS) Ch1 (does not count as a st), 8dc into the loop, sl st to join. Fasten off, leaving a 15cm tail for sewing.

Sew each circle onto the background square, adding 5-6 short stitches on one side.

Weave in ends.

LONG AND SKINNY

Using **245 (Green Yellow)**, ch26. Fasten off, leaving a 10cm tail for sewing. Sew the ch onto the background square, coiling it around so it loops and curves.

Weave in ends.

   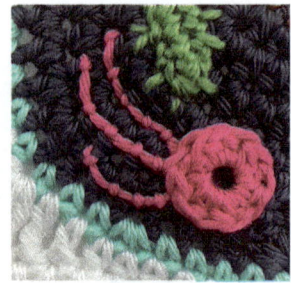

LADDER WHATSIT
Using **511 (Cornflower)**, ch9.

Row 1 (RS) Tr in fourth ch from hook, (ch1, skip st, tr in next st) twice, ch2. Fasten off, leaving a 15cm tail for sewing.

Sew onto the background square, adding short stitches at one end for legs.

Weave in ends.

DOUGHNUT WITH TENTACLES
Using **114 (Shocking Pink)**, make a magic loop.

Rnd 1 (RS) Ch2 (does not count as a st), 10htr into the loop, sl st to top of ch2 to join. Fasten off, leaving a 20cm tail for sewing.

Sew the ring onto the background square, adding three long curving stitches on one side. Secure each line with 4-5 little tacking stitches along its length.

Weave in ends.

SURFACE CROCHET
Using (254) Moon Rock:
1. Start with hook on RS of background square and yarn on WS. Insert hook into a space between sts and pull up a loop.
2. Insert hook into next space along. Yarn round hook.
3. Draw loop through to RS and through loop on hook. 1 st made.
4. Work 3-4 sts and fasten off. Repeat to work 4 tendrils.

Weave in ends.

CENTIPEDE THINGY
Using **412 (Forest Green)**, ch9.

Row 1 (RS) Dc in second ch from hook and in each ch to end. [8 sts]

Fasten off, leaving a 20cm tail for sewing.

Sew onto the background square, working a series of small stitches for legs around the edge, and two longer stitches for antennae. Add a French knot at the end of each antenna (see *Techniques* on page 13).

Weave in ends.

ZOOPLANKTON.

RANDOM EMBROIDERY STITCHES
Embroidery stitches make great zooplankton.

1. Cross stitch using **179 (Topaz)**
2. Straight stitch star using **281 (Tangerine)**
3. French knots using **Maxi Sweet Treat 074 (Mercury)**
4. Lazy daisy stitch using **Maxi Sweet Treat 404 (English Tea)**

Weave in ends.

WHAT IS ZOOPLANKTON?
Zooplankton is the collective name for tiny little organisms that drift around in the ocean. They include small creatures, such as diatoms and krill, and the immature stages of larger animals, such as the eggs and larvae of crustaceans, sea urchins and marine worms. Zooplankton is an integral part of the food chain.

Finishing Off.

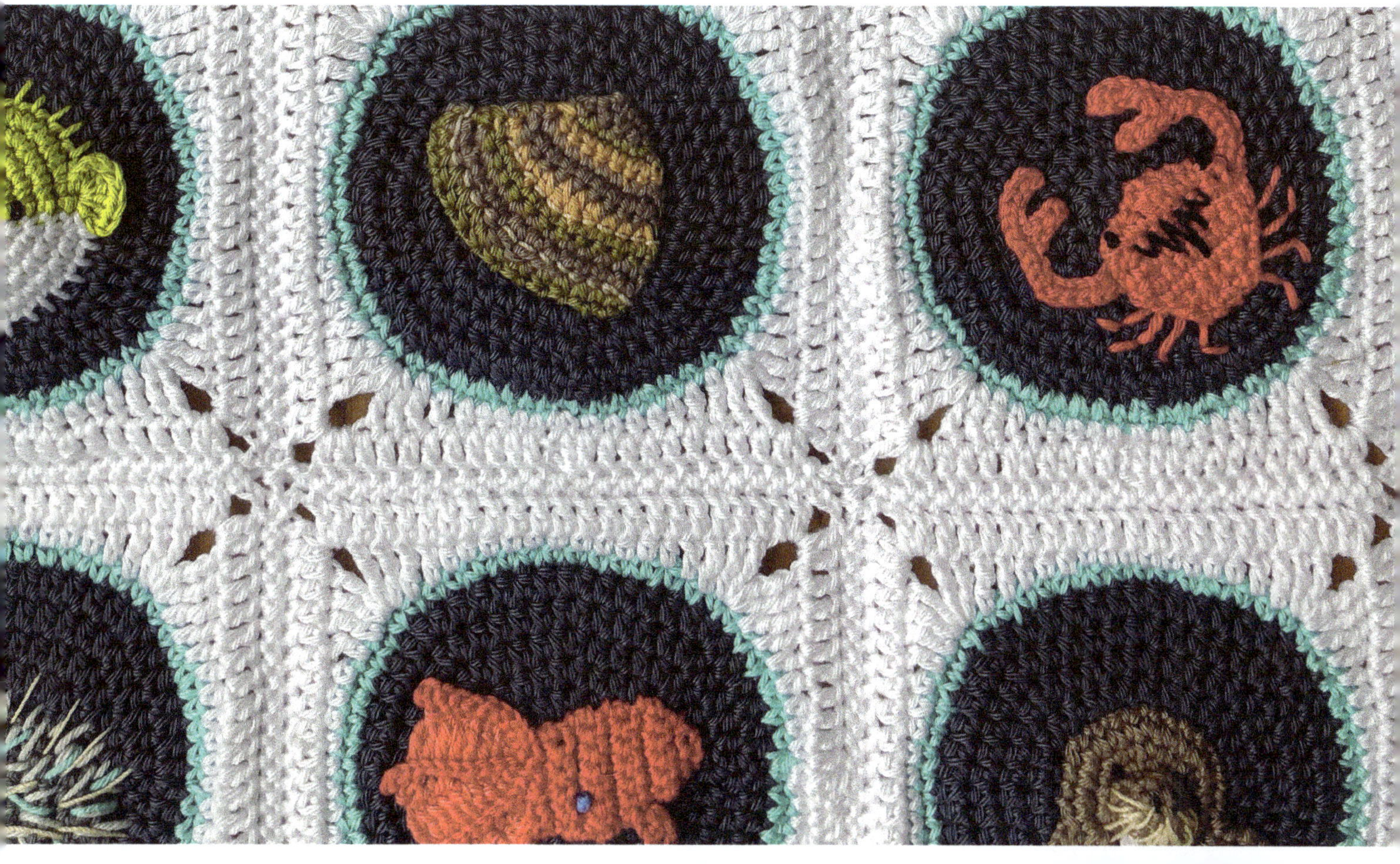

FINISHING OFF.

BLOCKING YOUR SQUARES.

For uniformity and nice crisp corners, block your squares before you sew down the creatures. Each square is designed to measure 12cm x 12cm (4¾ in x 4¾ in).

Pin out each square to measurements on a blocking board or folded towels. Pump steam onto it with a medium-hot iron held above (not touching) the square, or alternatively spritz with water until lightly damp and set aside

Once completely dry, unpin your square.

SEWING DOWN CREATURES.

- Arrange your squares so the seams on the background squares all run the same way; mine are all positioned vertically in the middle bottom.
- For big shapes (bodies, heads) use the first technique outlined here. For small or skinny areas the second technique will give you a tidier finish.
- Some creatures are well-suited to stuffing. Sew down the edges, leaving a small section unstitched. Insert a pinch of polyester stuffing into the space between the creature and the background square, and finish sewing the edge closed.
- Leave fins, tails and tentacles loose for added dimension to your squares.

TO SEW DOWN A BIG SHAPE
Use the same colour yarn as your shape. I've used a contrasting colour in the photos below.

1. Insert needle from WS up through background square and through the first st of creature. You want the two sts you're working through to be aligned directly above each other.
2. Reinsert needle back down into the same place.
3. Pull tight to finish the stitch.
4. Moving along to the next st on your creature, repeat steps 1-3. Your needle may need to pierce the background square stitches, or work into the end rows of the shape.

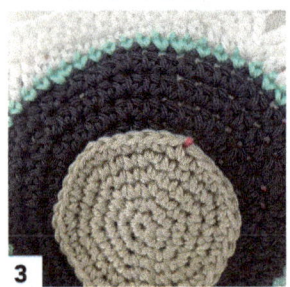 

TO SEW DOWN A SMALL SHAPE
For a small or skinny shape, it's easier to work a simple running stitch down the middle of the shape.

ATTACHING FABRIC BACKING.

Sewing down your creatures leaves a lot of exposed stitching on the back of your squares. To hide this, you can cover it with fabric circles, blanket-stitching them on. From the front, the blanket stitches are indistinguishable from the crochet stitches. Choose a soft fabric that won't fray. I've used a lightweight cotton sweatshirt material here, fluffy side out. You could also use a light wool or a thin polarfleece.

CUT OUT CIRCLES

1. Find a circle to use as a guide, like a bowl or cup (I used a Thunderbirds mug I found at the back of a cupboard — F.A.B, Virgil). You could also cut out a circle of cardboard. Your guide needs to cover the circle in the middle of the background square: just the tips of the Tropic sts should be exposed.
2. Use tailor's chalk to mark out 26 circles on the WS of your fabric.
3. Cut out your circles. I didn't bother covering the back of the corner squares because they didn't have any stitching to conceal. You could if you wish.
4. The cut-out circle.

BLANKET STITCHING

The next step is to attach the circles to your squares with blanket stitch, using **253 (Tropic)** and a tapestry needle.

1. Lay your circle over the WS of the background square. Insert your needle from the RS up into the space at the top of a Tropic st.
2. Work into the next Tropic st along. Reinsert your needle through the fabric circle down into the background square into the space at the bottom of the Tropic st. Bring your needle back up to into the space at the top of the same Tropic st.
3. Catch your needle under the first st made and draw yarn through. One blanket stitch made.
4. Repeat steps 2-3.
5. Continue blanket stitching around the circle. Aim for even placement of blanket stitches; you may need to skip a crochet stitch every now and then. When you get back to the start, work a stitch back into the first stitch. Fasten off and weave in ends.
6. This is a section of blanket stitches from the front.

Well-hidden, aren't they?

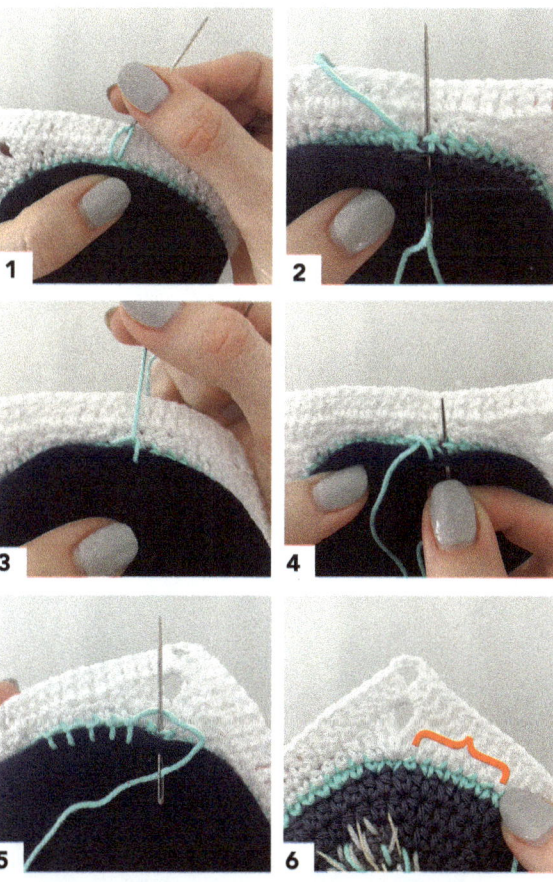

FINISHING OFF.

JOINING YOUR SQUARES.

The joining method featured here (dc seams on the wrong side) is a good one because it is quick, neat and easy. But feel free to join your squares with any method you prefer.

Switch to a 4mm (US G/6) hook, which will help you maintain a looser yet even tension. The dc sts are worked through the two inner loops only. This forms a strong seam that doesn't add too much bulk. At the corners, work into the chs rather than into the ch-sp.

Using **106 (Snow White)** (I've used a contrast colour in the photos below), line up two squares with WS facing out.

1. Start at the corner ch-3 sp. On each square, insert hook into ch adjacent to tr. Pull up a loop and ch1 (counts as one dc).
2. Insert hook into two innermost loops of next st on each square (BLO of front square and FLO of back square) and work a dc. Continue working a line of dc along the edge of the squares in this way.
3. The last st is worked into the first ch of the corner ch-3 sp.
4. Line up the next two squares and repeat steps 1-3. At the end of each row, fasten off. Work all seams in one direction first (either horizontally or vertically).

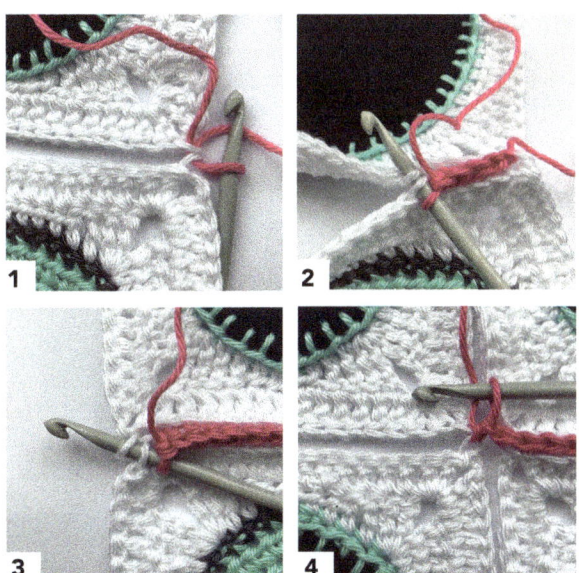

5. The seam from the front.

SEAMS IN THE OTHER DIRECTION

The seams in the other direction are worked in the same way. When you come to an intersection with a seam:

6. After the last dc, ch1. Work a dc around the seam by inserting your hook under the seam to draw up a loop.
7. Continue the seam in the usual way, working the next st in the chs as per step 4.

Weave in all ends, then lightly press the seams with a dry iron and a damp cloth on the WS. Take care not to iron the creatures in the process as it will flatten them.

FINISHING OFF.

WORKING THE BORDER.

A simple border is worked using the colours of the background squares and a 3mm hook. Again, feel free to use a different or more elaborate border if you want to. For a neater finish, fasten off each row with an invisible st before rejoining a new colour (see *Techniques* on pages 14 and 15).

Using **106 (Snow White)**, join yarn at any corner.

Rnd 1 Ch3 in the first tr after the corner ch-3 sp (does not count as a st throughout), tr in same st and in each st along side of first square.

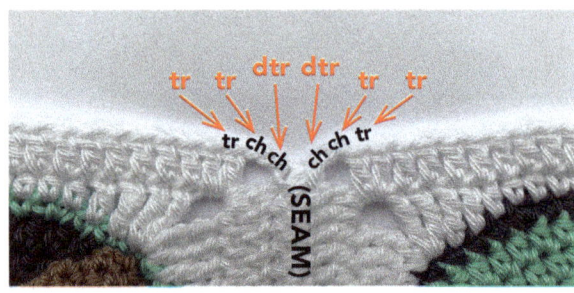

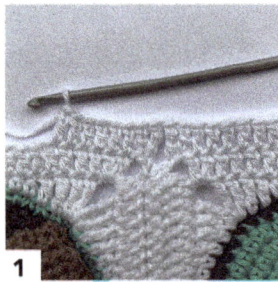 

1. At the end of the first square, tr in last tr, tr in first ch of corner ch-3 sp, dtr in second ch, skip seam; on the next square, dtr in first ch of corner ch-3 sp, tr in second ch, tr in first tr and in each st along side.
2. At the corners of the blanket, work (2tr, ch2, 2tr) around the ch-3 sp.

Repeat steps 1-2 around the edge of the blanket. Fasten off with an invisible st and weave in ends.

Rnd 2
Using **253 (Tropic)**, join yarn in BLO of first tr after corner ch-2 sp.

Ch1, BLO dc in same st and in each st around edge. Work blanket corners as Rnd 1 (2sts, ch2. 2sts), using dc. Once rnd complete, fasten off with an invisible st and weave in ends.

Rnd 3
Using **Snow White**, join yarn in BLO of first dc after corner ch-2 sp.

Ch3, BLO tr in same st and in each st around. Work blanket corners as Rnd 1, using tr. Once rnd complete, fasten off with an invisible st and weave in ends.

Rnd 4
Using **393 (Charcoal)**, join yarn in BLO of first tr after corner ch-2 sp.

Ch2, BLO htr in same st and in each st around. Work blanket corners as Rnd 1, using htr. Once rnd complete, fasten off with an invisible st and weave in ends.

Rnd 5
Using **Snow White**, join yarn in BLO of first htr after corner ch-2 sp.

Ch1, BLO dc in same st and in each st around edge. Work blanket corners as Rnd 1, using dc. Once rnd complete, fasten off with an invisible st and weave in ends.

Rnd 6
Using **Charcoal**, join yarn in BLO of first dc after corner ch-2 sp.

Ch3, BLO tr in same st and in each st around edge. Work blanket corners as Rnd 1, using tr. Once rnd complete, sl st into second tr. Do not cut yarn.

Rnd 7
Ch1, dc (both loops) in same st and in each st around edge. At corners, skip st either side of ch-2 sp and work corners as per Rnd 1.

Once rnd complete, fasten off with an invisible st and weave in ends.

Using a dry iron and a damp cloth, lightly press border on WS.

USING YOUR CREATURES.

If you're using the creatures as appliqué motifs, they will benefit from being blocked too (see page 68).

To make a brooch, use matching colour yarn and a tapestry needle to stitch a safety pin or brooch clasp to the back of the creature. Work little stitches and check the RS to make sure the stitches aren't visible on the front.

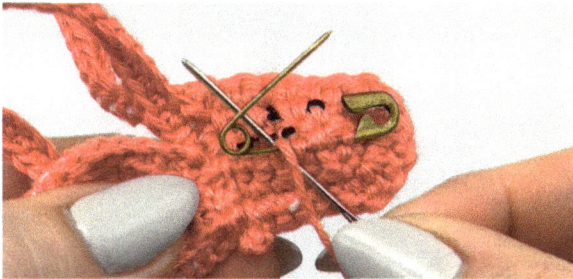

If you're making a fridge magnet, you could use hot glue to attach a small magnet to the WS but be careful. Use glue sparingly so it doesn't squeeze up through the stitches onto the RS. You can avoid glue-through by cutting a piece of felt into a shape slightly larger than the magnet. Glue the magnet to the felt shape, let it dry then stitch the felt to the creature.

HOORAY.
YOU'RE DONE!

FINISHING OFF.

Addendum.

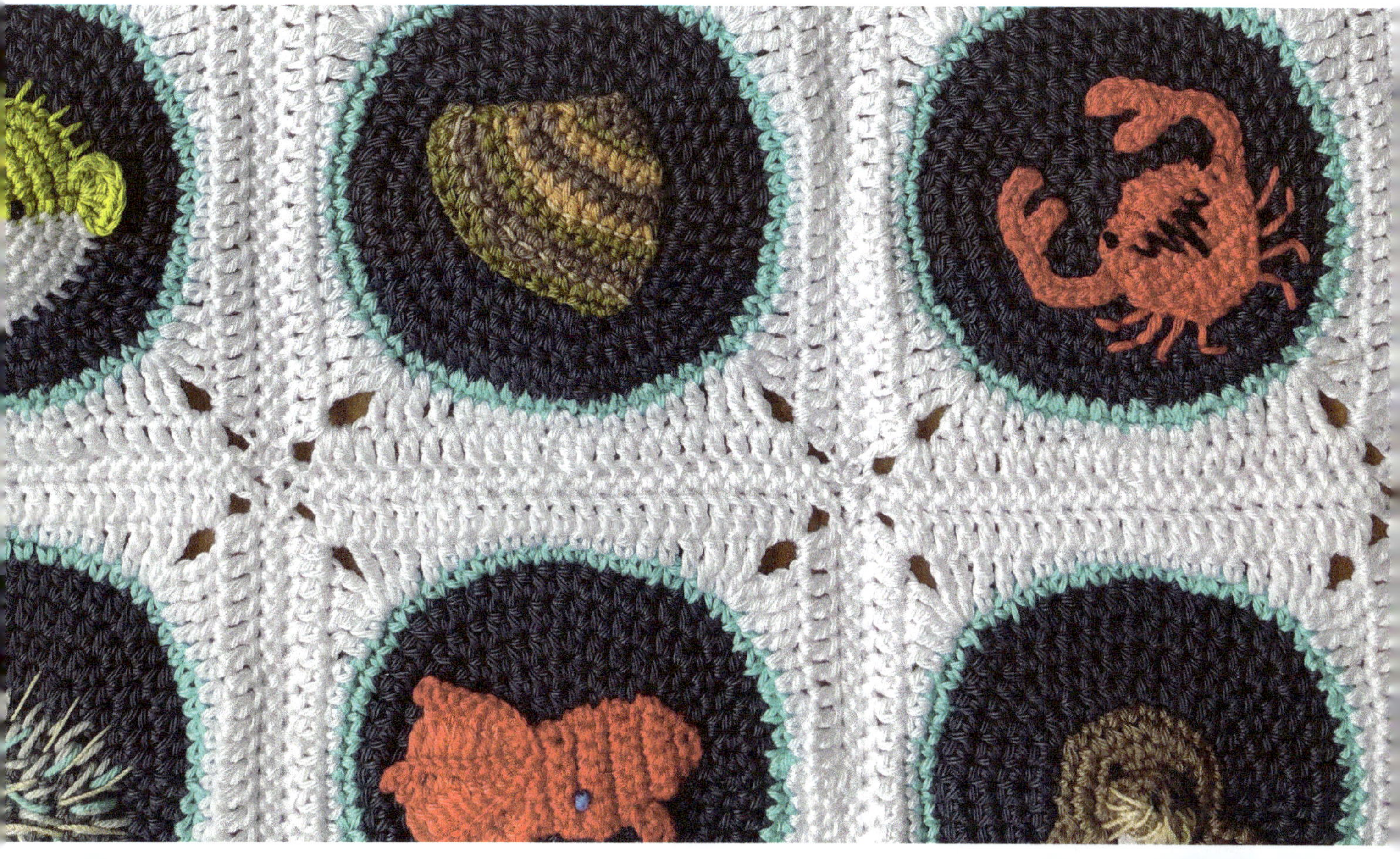

ADDENDUM // COLOURS REQUIRED.

The yarn used for this project is Scheepjes Catona, a fingering weight mercerised cotton. It's the best. Great stitch definition, lovely to work with and the biggest range of colours out there. And, conveniently for colour-hungry projects like this, Catona comes in smaller ball sizes. Some of the creatures also include details embroidered in Scheepjes Maxi Sweet Treat, a mercerised cotton laceweight yarn.

Below is a table of the Scheepjes colours you will need to make your A-B-Sea blanket and each creature.

Catona (100% cotton, 50g/125m)
Maxi Sweet Treat (100% cotton, 25g/140m)

STOCKISTS (WORLDWIDE DELIVERY)
www.woolwarehouse.co.uk
www.deramores.com
www.blacksheepwools.com

For a full list of retailers visit **www.scheepjes.com**

COLOUR	USED WHERE?	AMOUNT REQ'D
CATONA		**50g BALLS**
393 (Charcoal)	• All 30 background squares • Border	4
253 (Tropic)	• All 30 background squares • Blanket-stitching 26 squares • Border • Urchin	2
106 (Snow White)	• All 30 background squares • Border • Anemone • Clownfish • Great White Shark • Humuhumunukunukuapua'a • Inexplicable Shrimpgoby • Narwhal • Manta Ray • Porcupine Puffer • Tube Worms • Walrus	5 NB: 106 (Snow White) is available in 100g balls too. You would need: 2 x 100g balls 1 x 50g ball
		10g BALLS
516 (Candy Apple)	• Anemone • Red Crab • Vampire Squid	1
280 (Lemon)	• Anemone • Yellow Tang • Deep Sea Angler • Humuhumunukunukuapua'a	1

ADDENDUM: COLOURS REQUIRED.

COLOUR	USED WHERE?	AMOUNT REQ'D
CATONA		**10g BALLS**
518 (Marshmallow)	• Anemone • Blobfish • Jellyfish • Tube Worms	1
408 (Old Rose)	• Blobfish • Axolotl • Zooplankton	1
281 (Tangerine)	• Clownfish • Sea Slug • Zooplankton	1
507 (Chocolate)	• Deep Sea Angler • Loggerhead Sea Turtle	1
254 (Moon Rock)	• Deep Sea Angler • Electric Eel • Quahog • Walrus • Zooplankton	1
208 (Yellow Gold)	• Electric Eel • Humuhumunukunukuapua'a • Sea Slug	1
395 (Willow)	• Electric Eel • Quahog	1
114 (Shocking Pink)	• Jellyfish • Tube Worms • Axolotl • Zooplankton	1
511 (Cornflower)	• Flying Fish • Sea Slug • Vampire Squid • Zooplankton	1
172 (Pale Silver)	• Flying Fish • Great White Shark • Inexplicable Shrimpgoby • Narwhal • Urchin	1
110 (Black)	• Great White Shark • Humuhumunukunukuapua'a • Sea Slug	1

COLOUR	USED WHERE?	AMOUNT REQ'D
CATONA		**10g BALL**
397 (Cyan)	• Humuhumunukunukuapua'a • Zooplankton	1
412 (Forest Green)	• Kelp • Zooplankton	1
179 (Topaz)	• Loggerhead Sea Turtle • Quahog • Zooplankton	1
242 (Metal Grey)	• Manta Ray • Narwhal • Urchin	1
252 (Watermelon)	• Octopus • Vampire Squid	1
245 (Green Yellow)	• Porcupine Puffer • Yellow Tang • Zooplankton	1
MAXI SWEET TREAT		**25g BALL**
106 (Black)	• Eyes for 16 creatures	1
238 (Powder Pink)	• Octopus • Great White Shark	1
074 (Mercury)	• Flying Fish • Inexplicable Shrimpgoby • Manta Ray • Zooplankton	1
404 (English Tea)	• Loggerhead Sea Turtle • Quahog • Urchin • Zooplankton	1

TOTAL YARN REQUIRED	
Catona 50g	11 balls
Catona 10g	19 balls
Maxi Sweet Treat 25g	4 balls

ADDENDUM: COLOURS REQUIRED.

ABOUT.

HI TEAM!

I'm Pony McTate, a crochet designer from New Zealand. I make things that are fun and bold, contemporary and playful. Unconventional? Yes. Fabulous? Always. I've been creative from a young age but I only picked up a crochet hook a few years ago. It really clicked for me. All of a sudden I could make stuff, quickly, that was both practical and cool.

Now I design regularly for magazines, yarn companies and for my pattern shop. You can check out my work on the channels below.

I live in the countryside high on a hill with my husband and our two wee boys. I find innovative places to store my yarn. Our cat Stampy likes to get involved in everything, which is lovely at times, and at other times.... less so. I mean, she likes to roll around in glitter. Oh look, surprise surprise, there she is down there.

ACKNOWLEDGMENTS

Special thanks to two crochet superstars (and all round good eggs), Kate Bruning of @greedyforcolour and Shelley Husband of @spincushions, who gave me cheerful advice, tech support and soothing consolation when it all got too much. My lovely test crocheters whipped out lots of fishy goodness in record time. My grateful thanks also to Scheepjes who jumped on board with yarn support after I approached them about my bonkers idea. And a big ol' hug to my poor neglected family, who put up with blobfish on the bed, tube worms on the table and electric eels everywhere else for a very, very long time. xx

FIND ME HERE.

- Instagram: @ponymctate
- Facebook: @ponymctate
- Etsy: ponymctate
- Ravelry: ponymctate
- Pinterest: ponymctate
- Email: pony@ponymctate.com

Use the hashtag

#CrochetABSea

when you share your make!

www.ponymctate.com

www.ingramcontent.com/pod-product-compliance
Lightning Source LLC
Chambersburg PA
CBHW061754290426
44108CB00029B/2997